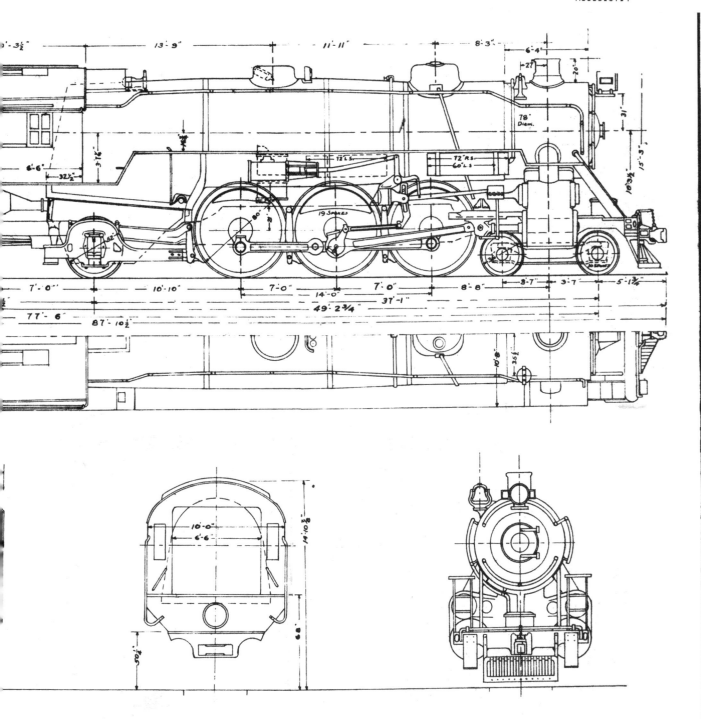

No. & Diam.	212 - 2¼"	TENDER		
	40 · 5½"			
OVER SHEETS	19·0"	" CAP'Y COAL	19½ TON	
PONY TRUCK	63 000 LBS.	" " WATER	11000 GAL.	
DRIVERS	201 000 "	" DECK	178"	
L	326000 "	TRACTIVE FORCE	50.000 LBS.	

THE BALTIMORE & OHIO R. R. CO.

CLASS P-7 4-6-2

Nos. 5300 - 5319

PUBLIC RELATIONS DEPT.
BALTIMORE, MD

U- 1381

DR.	TR.	CHK.
G.F.N.	G.F.N.	G.F.N.

B&O Pacific Locomotives:
Handsome Passenger Workhorses

Bob Withers

Published 2013 by
TLC Publishing Inc.
18292 Forest Rd.
Forest, Virginia 24551
434-385-4076

ACKNOWLEDGEMENTS

The author thanks and dedicates this book to the late Jim Boyd, Thomas W. Dixon Jr., the late William D. Edson, Lloyd D. Lewis, the late Lawrence W. Sagle, F.M. Swengel, Alvin F. Staufer, the U.S. Department of Transportation's ICC Accident Investigation Archive, and all the photographers whose work is herein featured, without whose help this treatise on railroad history would not have been possible. Thanks are also due to Mike Cather, Ed Kirstatter, Gregory Smith, and Jim Mischke, all members of the B&O Railroad Historical Society, whose close review of the book in the late stages of its development significantly improved it.

ISBN 9780939487615

Library of Congress Control Number: 2013934453

Digital Photo Production, Layout and Design by
Karen Parker

Printed in the U.S.A. by
Walsworth Print Group, Marceline, Mo.

Cover Photo: Class P-7 Pacific 5311, the President Fillmore, takes Train 2, the eastbound National Limited, across the Thomas Viaduct at Relay, Md., in about 1936. Originally an all-Pullman train, by this time coaches are being permitted to hobnob with the sleepers. (H. W. Pontin Photo, TLC Collection, black and white photo colorized by Karen Parker)

Title Page: Class P-6a Pacific 5244 departs Kenova, W.Va., with Train 72 in 1956. The tiny B&O combination station is hidden behind the coach, but clearly visible is the elevated Norfolk & Western mainline and N&W / C&O Union Station just down the road. No. 5244 was the 15th and final P-6a. It headed the last run of Train 72 on January 31, 1957 before being retired in favor of new diesel passenger locomotives. (Herbert H. Harwood Jr. photo, Bob Withers Collection)

Opposite: Class P-1d Pacific 5003 charges through Patterson Creek, W.Va., on July 29, 1948, with an eastbound seven-car passenger train. The locomotive was converted from Class Q-1 Mikado 4017 in 1926. (R.H. Kindig, TLC Collection)

Back Cover Top: When the P-7 Pacifics were built, the B&O issued this illustration showing the new engine in all its striped glory. (Courtesy of Bill Howes)

Back Cover Bottom: The six-car Cincinnatian is seen here pulling into Toledo Union Station in 1954, led by streamlined class P-7d Pacific No. 5304. (Bob's Photo Collection)

Front End Sheets: The B&O Publicity Department issued this drawing of a P-7 Pacific as part of a set of significant B&O locomotives. (TLC Collection)

Back End Sheets: This B&O system map is taken from the May 16, 1937 public timetable. (TLC Collection)

Table of Contents

Introduction

This is the ninth book in the TLC B&O series:

- B&O Passenger Service, Vol. 1 (1993)

- B&O E-Units (1994)

- B&O Passenger Service, Vol. 2 (1997)

- B&O Cabooses (1998)

- Coal & Coke Railroad, a B&O Predecessor (2002)

- B&O Steam Locomotives, The last 30 Years (2003)

- B&O's Cincinnatian (2008)

- B&O's EM-1 2-8-8-4 Articulated Locomotive (2007)

- West Virginia Railroads, Vol. 3, B&O (2011)

This work also treats a particular type of locomotive and its use on the Baltimore & Ohio. In this case the focus is on the 4-6-2 Pacific type wheel arrangement. The B&O adopted this type in the first decade of the 20th Century, at the very outset of its popularity as a passenger-service locomotive type in the United States. By the end of the steam era the Pacific was probably the most popular of all locomotive classes that tended to be devoted strictly to passenger service. B&O used its Pacific types, classified "P-" on the company's mechanical rosters, on the majority of its passenger trains, from short 3- to 4-car secondary runs and branch line operations to the top of the line *Capitol Limited* and *National Limited*. The Pacific is associated with every era of B&O passenger train operations from the World War I period to the end of steam.

Possessing some of the best examples of the 4-6-2, B&O stands as one of the type's principal users, and is studied today by steam locomotive historians and aficionados, and modelers, as some of the best. Its flashy green-jacketed "Presidents" Pacifics occasioned much comment in their time. The streamlined engines designed for *The Cincinnatian* represent one of the better streamlined designs.

This book is by Bob Withers, a recognized B&O historian who has to his credit many books for TLC, Morning Sun, and other publishers. The book contains a detailed roster of all the B&O 4-6-2's, and some background about each class. The main thrust of the work, however, is in the photos presented, which are intended to represent the Pacifics in all types of work across the B&O system.

Thomas W. Dixon Jr.
March 2013

P-1aa No. 5044, arriving in Parkersburg, W. Va. with Train 23, the West Virginian, *trails a magnificent plume of steam and smoke in 1948. Judging by the number of head-end cars, this train must have done considerable mail and express business. (S. P. Davidson photo, Jay Williams Collection)*

A History of B&O Pacifics

Passenger locomotives of the 4-6-2 wheel arrangement had a little difficulty getting started. The first standard-gauge examples known to the author were three cross-compound engines built by the Rhode Island Locomotive Works for the Chicago, Milwaukee & St. Paul Railroad in 1893. CM&StP wasn't satisfied with them and returned them to the builder, which rebuilt them as simple engines and sold them to the Savannah, Florida & Western Railway. The SF&W was absorbed into the Atlantic Coast Line in 1902, and the ACL rebuilt the locomotives into 4-6-0 Ten Wheelers 10 years later.

One source says that, as early as 1888, there were a few Ten Wheelers that were rebuilt into the 4-6-2 type by adding a trailer truck, but the author has found no record of them.

The standard-gauge 4-6-2 type began in earnest with 13 Q-Class engines built by Baldwin Locomotive Works for the New Zealand Railways Department in 1901 (New Zealand had purchased a few narrow-gauge 4-6-2's in 1895) and similar power built by Brooks for Missouri Pacific and by the American Locomotive Company's Schenectady, N.Y., works for the Chesapeake & Ohio in 1902.

Builders developed the wheel arrangement after a Baldwin 2-4-2 Columbia was displayed at the World's Columbian Exposition in Chicago's Jackson Park in 1893, which introduced the idea of adding a trailer truck to steam locomotive designs to permit larger fireboxes and grate areas than were possible with 4-4-0 Americans and 4-6-0 Ten Wheelers. Larger and wider fireboxes could not be positioned over the driving wheels but could be accommodated by adding the trailing truck. With that added set of wheels and repositioned fireboxes, boilers also could be placed lower on the mainframes. In freight service, the 2-8-2 Mikado evolved from the 2-8-0 Consolidation for the same reasons.

Two explanations have been advanced to show why the 4-6-2 came to be called "Pacific." One claims the name was coined because the first one was shipped across the Pacific Ocean to New Zealand. The other derives from the fact that the first such engines built for an American carrier went to the Missouri Pacific. C&O received their Pacifics in August 1902, a few weeks after MoPac took delivery of its engines, so that railroad received all the publicity in trade journals.

Ever cautious and conservative, the Baltimore & Ohio Railroad waited several years to order its first 35 Pacifics, from Alco/Schenectady. Numbered 2100 to 2134, the Class P locomotives came equipped with 74-inch drivers, 22- by 28-inch cylinders, Stephenson valve gear and piston valves, and 210 pounds steam pressure. The piston valves were set at an angle to accommodate the Stephenson valve gear. The locomotives weighed 229,500 pounds and developed 32,690 pounds of tractive effort.

Missouri Pacific (top) and Chesapeake & Ohio (bottom) Pacific type locomotives, delivered just weeks apart in 1902. These were the first successful domestic locomotives of their wheel arrangement. They were followed by thousands of sisters on virtually every major railroad in the United States, including the B&O, which eventually rostered 277 locomotives of this type. (MP - Karen Parker Collection, C&O - Chesapeake & Ohio Historical Society Collection)

Alco builder's photo of B&O Class P No. 2100, B&O's first Pacific type locomotive, delivered in 1905. (Alco Historic Photos)

Despite the late start, B&O must have loved its Pacifics – eventually buying or refashioning from Mikados 277 of them. As long as steam lasted, they served as the company's passenger train workhorses. Because of the fact that the railroad neither bought nor built any 4-8-4's and developed only four 4-6-4 Hudsons, the terms "B&O passenger engine" and "Pacific" virtually were synonymous. Even after the advent of passenger diesels, Pacifics were used regularly as helpers in mountainous areas.

Other North American railroads liked them, too – buying or building more than 6,800 of them – amounting to 9 percent of total steam engine production in the United States and Canada.

In their early days, B&O Pacifics were given some choice assignments – such as first runs of legendary trains such as the *Capitol Limited* and *National Limited*. Several of them were selected to pull trains for the President of the United States – a topic that will be dealt with later in this book.

As the company acquired newer and more powerful locomotives, older and smaller models were shifted to other territories and assignments. For example, the 1927 arrival of the P-7 class relegated the P-6 class to the Akron and Chicago divisions. Then, when diesels began hauling main line trains, the P-7 class went to the Cumberland, Chicago and Toledo divisions. The powerful P-1d engines worked on the Cumberland, Pittsburgh, Monongah and Wheeling divisions – mostly in mountainous areas – while smaller P-3 and P-4 locomotives mainly protected commuter service in the Pittsburgh and Washington-Baltimore areas until Rail Diesel Cars took over in 1953.

The light USRA P-5 class ended up on the Ohio and St. Louis divisions, and took over runs on the West End of the Wheeling Division's Ohio River subdivision once completion of a new Kanawha River Bridge at Point Pleasant, W.Va., in 1947 permitted replacement of tiny Class B-8 Ten Wheelers.

As B&O's diesel onslaught intensified, Pacifics were bumped from the major passenger trains to secondary, local and branch line runs. As those trains were discontinued, most of the Pacifics went to scrap – but some hung around long enough to be assigned to freight trains, mixed trains and work trains.

The only Pacifics to survive until B&O's Nov. 1, 1956, renumbering plan – which was designed to vacate four-digit number series to make room for the ever-increasing number of diesels – included three from the P-6a class and 17 from the P-7 class. At least, that is, officially. A few Pacifics not assigned new numbers were observed operating after their alleged out-of-service dates, and the author suspects that others never received their assigned new numbers before they were removed from service. Details also will unfold later in this book.

Occasionally, those surviving Pacifics substituted for diesels that ran into trouble. When Train 54, the northbound *Cincinnatian*, struck an automobile in Dayton, Ohio, on May 2, 1957, officers cut off the lead unit, replaced it with passenger GP9 3407, and replaced it on another train with Class P-7e Pacific 114 (former 5316).

For railroading in general, Pacifics remained popular longer than many people realize. The last locomotive of that wheel arrangement in North America was built by the Canadian Locomotive Company for Canadian Pacific in 1948. Worldwide, the most recent one known to the author is the 60163, *Tornado*, built in 2008 by the A1 Steam Locomotive Trust (a railway preservation organization) in Darlington, England.

Alas, only one of B&O's Pacifics still exists. Class P-7 5300, the former *President Washington*, is on display today at the B&O Railroad Museum in Baltimore.

Summary Roster of B&O Pacific Locomotives			
Class	*Number Series*	*Quantity*	*Built*
Locomotives Built for the B&O			
P	5150-5184	35	1905-1906
P-1, P-1a	5050-5089	40	1911
P-1c	5000-5009 5035-5049 5090-5094	30	1924-1926 Rebuilt from older 2-8-2s
P-3	5100-5129	30	1913
P-4	5130-5139	10	1917-1918
P-5	5200-5229	30	1919
P-6	5230-5244	15	1922
P-7	5300-5319	20	1927
P-9	5320	1	1928
	Total	211	
Locomotives Obtained via Merger			
P-2	5095-5099	5	ex CH&D
P-8	5196-5199	4	ex CI&W
P-10	5265	1	Alton, ex C&A
P-11	5266	1	Alton, ex C&A
P-12	5267-5269	3	Alton, ex C&A
P-13	5270-5274	5	Alton, ex C&A
P-14	5275-5279	5	Alton, ex C&A
P-15	5280-5289	10	Alton, ex C&A
P-16	5290-5299	10	Alton, ex C&A
P-17	5140-5148	9	ex BR&P
P-18	5185-5192	8	ex BR&P
P-19	5260-5264	5	ex BR&P
	Total	66	
	Grand Total	277	

No matter how efficient they were and how well they did the jobs for which they were designed, B&O Pacifics also suffered their share of fatal derailments. Here's a sampling:

• March 26, 1919: Class Pa Pacific 5032 derailed as it was crossing over from the eastbound main to the west leg of a wye at Laughlin Junction, Pa., near Pittsburgh, damaging switch points and bending or breaking connecting rods. Repairs were in process when a light engine, backing to the Smithfield Street Station to pick up a train, moved into the crossover because officers had failed to stop it and sideswiped an outbound passenger train. Eight passengers and one employee were killed and 81 passengers and six employees were injured.

• June 30, 1950: Class P-7d 5301 and Class P-1d 5048, at the head end of westbound 16-car mail-and-express Train 29, struck a broken rail inside a tunnel near Eaton, W.Va., derailing both engines and the first six cars. The derailed engines skidded along the tunnel's north wall, damaging it, and once outside, turned over. The 5048's engineer was killed; the other engineer and both firemen were injured. Ironically, the 5301 was working its way west to begin hauling the former Baltimore-Cincinnati *Cincinnatian* on its new Cincinnati-Detroit route.

• April 5, 1952: Class P-1d 5041, pulling Connellsville, Pa.-Grafton, W.Va., Train 66, struck a broken rail near Kingmont, W.Va., overturning the engine and derailing all three cars. The engineer died and the fireman, conductor, baggageman, flagman and two passengers were hurt.

• February 11, 1953: Class P-7e 5316, pulling an eight-car Train 23, the *West Virginian*, struck an automobile on the Summit Avenue crossing in Gaithersburg, Md., killing all four occupants inside. The locomotive, tender and first seven cars were derailed and the locomotive turned over. The engineer, fireman, baggageman and 10 passengers were injured.

• April 17, 1953: Class P-1d 5049, pulling a westbound 10-car troop train, overturned a rail near Smithburg, W.Va., derailing the engine and the first seven cars. The engineer died and the fireman was hurt.

The P Class Pacifics

American Locomotive Company's Schenectady Works delivered the original 35 P-series locomotives, Nos. 2100-2134, between December 1905 and April 1906. They were renumbered into the 5000-5034 series in 1918 and again to the 5150-5184 series in 1926.

Thirteen of the engines received superheaters and were reclassified as Pa. Outside valves were added to 19 others when they were superheated, and Walschaert valve gear was applied to two and Baker valve gear to 17, which became Classes Pb and Pc respectively. In fact, the company modified so many of the series that by 1930, only three remained as built. But, all the improvements aside, they were all gone by the end of 1949.

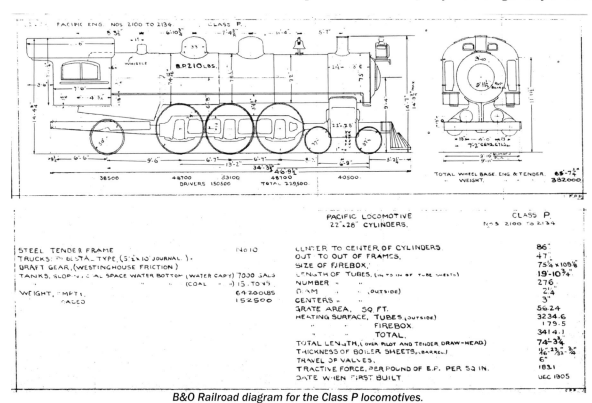

B&O Railroad diagram for the Class P locomotives.

Class P No. 2107 has stopped with its train on the Royal Blue Line between Washington, D.C., and Jersey City, N.J. (New York City) so the photographer can take its picture, probably sometime in 1906 when the locomotive was new from Alco. (B&O Railroad photo, TLC Collection)

Class P Roster						
Orig Number	2nd Number	3rd number	Built	Builder	Rebuilt	Retired
2100	5000	5150	Dec-05	Alco-Schenectady	Pa	1937
2101	5001	5151	Mar-06	Alco-Schenectady	Pa	1937
2102	5002	5152	Mar-06	Alco-Schenectady	Pa	1937
2103	5003	5153	Mar-06	Alco-Schenectady	Pb	1947
2104	5004	5154	Mar-06	Alco-Schenectady	Pb	1947
2105	5005	5155	Mar-06	Alco-Schenectady		1937
2106	5006	5156	Mar-06	Alco-Schenectady	Pa, Pb	1947
2107	5007	5157	Mar-06	Alco-Schenectady	Pa	1939
2108	5008	5158	Mar-06	Alco-Schenectady	Pc	1947
2109	5009	5159	Mar-06	Alco-Schenectady	Pa	1937
2110	5010	5160	Mar-06	Alco-Schenectady	Pa	1937
2111	5011	5161	Mar-06	Alco-Schenectady	Pc	1947
2112	5012	5162	Mar-06	Alco-Schenectady	Pc	1938
2113	5013	5163	Mar-06	Alco-Schenectady		1937
2114	5014	5164	Mar-06	Alco-Schenectady	Pa, Pc	1947
2115	5015	5165	Mar-06	Alco-Schenectady	Pc	1947
2116	5016	5166	Apr-06	Alco-Schenectady	Pa	1937
2117	5017	5167	Apr-06	Alco-Schenectady		1937
2118	5018	5168	Apr-06	Alco-Schenectady	Pa, Pc	1949
2119	5019	5169	Apr-06	Alco-Schenectady	Pa	1946
2120	5020	5170	Apr-06	Alco-Schenectady	Pc	1949
2121	5021	5171	Apr-06	Alco-Schenectady	Pa, Pc	1947
2122	5022	5172	Apr-06	Alco-Schenectady	Pa, Pc	1949
2123	5023	5173	Apr-06	Alco-Schenectady	Pc	1947
2124	5024	5174	Apr-06	Alco-Schenectady	Pa	1937
2125	5025	5175	Apr-06	Alco-Schenectady	Pc	1942
2126	5026	5176	Apr-06	Alco-Schenectady	Pc	1947
2127	5027	5177	Apr-06	Alco-Schenectady	Pc	1947
2128	5028	5178	Apr-06	Alco-Schenectady	Pa, Pc	1948
2129	5029	5179	Apr-06	Alco-Schenectady	Pa	1937
2130	5030	5180	Apr-06	Alco-Schenectady	Pa, Pc	1947
2131	5031	5181	Apr-06	Alco-Schenectady	Pa	1941
2132	5032	5182	Apr-06	Alco-Schenectady	Pa	1937
2133	5033	5183	Apr-06	Alco-Schenectady	Pc	1947
2134	5034	5184	Apr-06	Alco-Schenectady	Pc	1948

Notes:

Class Pa was superheated and retained the Stephenson valve gear and inside piston valves.

Class Pb was superheated and equipped with Walschaert valve gear and outside piston valves.

Class Pc was superheated and equipped with Baker valve gear and outside piston valves.

All rebuilds were done in the B&O shops.

Class P No. 5167 rests with its stack covered in Cleveland, Ohio, in May 1930. This engine is one of only three that were never rebuilt, the only change from her as-built appearance being a new smaller cab and a different design trailing truck (See page 6 for comparison). (Jerry Miller Collection)

Aside from the new cab, class Pa No. 5181 looks pretty much as she did when she was built. The real change was inside the front of the boiler, which now contains a superheater. (Bud Laws Collection)

The Baker valve gear tells us that No. 5183 is a class Pc. In addition to new cylinders and valve gear, the engine has received a superheater. The tender, too, is different – one of B&O's novel "dump" tenders, whose coal bunkers would tilt up to help move the coal toward the fireman. Seen in Washington, D.C., on August 20, 1945. (Jerry Miller Collection)

No. 5165, another class Pc, is seen here in 1940 in Youngstown, Ohio. (Bud Laws Collection)

Class Pc No. 5184 doubleheads with another Pacific on a passenger train sometime in the 1930s. Note that the second engine is equipped with a Vanderbilt tender, indicating it is either a P-4 or P-6. (Bud Laws Collection)

The P-1 Class Pacifics

Baldwin built B&O's 10 Class P-1 Pacifics, Nos. 2135-2144, in 1911. They were greatly improved over their predecessors. Weighing 271,040 pounds and capable of developing 43,400 pounds of tractive effort and 205 pounds steam pressure, they came equipped with 74-inch drivers, 24x32 inch cylinders and Walschaerts valve gear. They were renumbered in 1918 to the 5050-5059 series.

Later in 1911, Baldwin built 30 Class P-1a Pacifics for B&O, numbered 2145-2174. They differed from the previous batch only by weighing 277,190 pounds and being delivered with superheaters. They were transferred to the 5060-5089 series in 1918.

Beginning in 1913, engines of the original P-1 class received superheaters and were reclassed as P-1a. When all 40 locomotives received 26x32 inch cylinders and outside steam pipes, they became Class P-1aa. They now weighed 277,190 pounds and were rated at 47,300 pounds tractive effort and 190 pounds steam pressure.

B&O's Mount Clare Shops in Baltimore kept tinkering with the P-1 classes for years. Class P-1b locomotives were converted from Class P-1a starting in 1919, with 26x28 inch cylinders, 299,000 pounds weight and 44,600 pounds tractive effort. The 5059 received long-travel Baker valve gear. Class P-1ba, with the same specs as P-1b, were converted from P-1 and P-1a locomotives, beginning in 1924.

Also starting in 1924, B&O began rebuilding Class Q-1a, Q-1aa, Q-1b and Q-1ba Mikados into Class P-1c and P-1ca Pacifics. Specs were identical to Classes P-1b and P-1ba. The 5043 was equipped with a booster, which raised its weight to 309,000 pounds and tractive effort to 55,600 pounds. The 5094 received long-travel Baker valve gear.

Four years later, Mount Clare began building Class P-1d Pacifics from earlier models – including P-1aa, P-1b, P-1ba and P-1c. The P-1d class featured 26½x28 inch cylinders, 74-inch drivers, 318,500 pounds weight, 51,000 pounds tractive effort, and 225 pounds steam pressure. Some of the engines were equipped with water-tube fireboxes, as shown in the adjacent tables, and one had a booster for a while.

The P-1d class had large, square-tank tenders that carried 21 tons of coal and 13,500 gallons of water, Walschaerts valve gear, stokers and power reverse gears. Some had water scoops. The class was efficient, and comprised B&O's most powerful Pacific class.

P-1c and P-1d locomotives hauled most B&O passenger trains over the mountains. During the 1940s and '50s, the engine waiting at Cumberland, Md., for the westbound *Capitol Limited*, or at Keyser, W.Va., for the westbound *National Limited*, most likely would be a P-1c or P-1d. The helper waiting at Piedmont and Rowlesburg, W.Va., or Hyndman, Pa., unless it were a Mikado, would most assuredly be a P-1c or P-1d. The last one, the 5044, was retired in November 1956 and scrapped at Parkersburg, W.Va.

Baldwin builder's photo of Class P-1 No. 2140, later renumbered to 5055. (TLC Collection)

			Class P-1 Roster		
1st Number	**2nd Number**	**Built**	**Rebuilt To Class**	**Retired**	**Comment**
2135	5050	Jan-11	P-1aa	1943	Rebuilt into T-3b No. 5565
2136	5051	Jan-11	P-1aa	Aug-51	
2137	5052	Jan-11	P-1aa, P-1d	1955	semi-watertube firebox P-1d
2138	5053	Jan-11	P-1b, P-1d	Jun-54	
2139	5054	Jan-11	P-1aa	Sep-52	
2140	5055	Jan-11	P-1aa	1943	Rebuilt into T-3b No. 5567
2141	5056	Jan-11	P-1aa, P-1b, P-1d	Mar-54	semi-watertube firebox P-1d
2142	5057	Jan-11	P-1aa	Apr-52	
2143	5058	Feb-11	P-1aa, P-1b, P-1d	Nov-53	
2144	5059	Feb-11	P-1aa, P-1b, P-1d	1956	semi-watertube firebox P-1d
2145	5060	Sep-11	P-1aa	Apr-52	
2146	5061	Sep-11	P-1aa, P-1d	Apr-52	semi-watertube firebox P-1d
2147	5062	Sep-11	P-1aa, P-1c	Dec-53	
2148	5063	Sep-11	P-1aa	1943	Rebuilt into T-3 No. 5560
2149	5064	Sep-11	P-1aa	1943	Rebuilt into T-3b No. 5566
2150	5065	Sep-11	P-1aa, P-1b, P-1c	Oct-53	
2151	5066	Sep-11	P-1aa, P-1b, P-1c	Mar-54	semi-watertube firebox P-1d
2152	5067	Sep-11	P-1aa	Sep-52	
2153	5068	Sep-11	P-1aa, P-1d	1955	semi-watertube firebox P-1d
2154	5069	Sep-11	P-1aa	Apr-52	
2155	5070	Sep-11	P-1aa, P-1d	1956	semi-watertube firebox P-1d
2156	5071	Sep-11	P-1a	1943	Rebuilt into T-3 No. 5559
2157	5072	Sep-11	P-1aa	Dec-52	
2158	5073	Sep-11	P-1aa	Jun-51	
2159	5074	Sep-11	P-1aa, P-1da	Dec-53	
2160	5075	Sep-11	P-1aa, P-1da	Dec-53	
2161	5076	Sep-11	P-1aa	Nov-52	
2162	5077	Sep-11	P-1aa	Apr-52	
2163	5078	Sep-11	P-1aa	Apr-52	
2164	5079	Sep-11	P-1aa	May-52	
2165	5080	Sep-11	P-1aa, P-1ba	Dec-53	
2166	5081	Sep-11	P-1aa	May-52	
2167	5082	Sep-11	P-1aa	Jun-52	
2168	5083	Sep-11	P-1aa, P-1ba, P-1d	1954	semi-watertube firebox P-1d
2169	5084	Sep-11	P-1aa, P-1d	Mar-54	
2170	5085	Sep-11	P-1aa, P-1ba, P-1d	1956	semi-watertube firebox P-1d
2171	5086	Sep-11	P-1aa, P-1d	1956	semi-watertube firebox P-1d
2172	5087	Sep-11	P-1aa, P-1ba, P-1d	Feb-51	
2173	5088	Oct-11	P-1aa	1945	Rebuilt into T-3b No. 5578
2174	5089	Oct-11	P-1aa, P-1ba	Dec-53	

All were built by Baldwin Locomotive Works.

When these Pacifics were rebuilt into class T-3 and T-3b 4-8-2s, only the boiler shell was used. The remainder of the locomotive was scrapped.

Number	Built	Rebuilt From 2-8-2	Rebuilt to	Retired	Comment
5035	1924	4031	P-1d	Jun-54	
5036	1924	4138	P-1d	Dec-54	
5037	1924	4217		1933	Destroyed in boiler explosion
5038	1924	4044	P-1d	1956	
5039	1924	4171		1956	
5040	1924	4203	P-1d	1956	semi-watertube firebox P-1d
5041	1924	4183	P-1d	Jan-54	
5042	1924	4136		Nov-53	
5043	1924	4111	P-1d	1956	
5044	1924	4181	P-1d	Nov-56	semi-watertube firebox P-1d
5045	1924	4149		Dec-53	
5046	1924	4172	P-1d	1956	
5047	1924	4182		1933	Rebuilt into V-1 4-6-4
5048	1925	4048	P-1d	Mar-54	
5049	1925	4120		1956	semi-watertube firebox P-1d
5090	1925	4006		1955	
5091	1925	4122	P-1d	1955	
5092	1925	4037	P-1d	Jun-54	
5093	1925	4063	P-1ca, P-1d	Jul-54	
5094	1925	4034	P-1ca, P-1d	Mar-54	
5000	1926	4076	P-1da	Nov-50	
5001	1926	4091		1956	
5002	1926	4126		Nov-53	
5003	1926	4017	P-1d	Jul-54	semi-watertube firebox P-1d
5004	1926	4105		Dec-53	
5005	1926	4110		1955	
5006	1926	4107		Nov-53	
5007	1926	4106		Dec-53	
5008	1926	4137		Nov-53	
5009	1926	4119		Jul-54	

All were rebuilt into 4-6-2's from 2-8-2's at the B&O's Mt. Clare Shops.

Class P-1c Roster

B&O Railroad diagram for class P-1c locomotives.

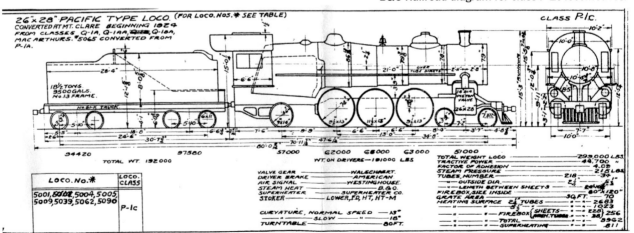

14

Class	Cylinders (bore x stroke inches)	Driver Diameter (inches)	Weight (pounds)	Tractive Effort (pounds)	Boiler Pressure (pounds per square inch)	Valve Gear	Notes
P-1	24x32	74	271,040	43,400	205	W	built new
P-1a	24x32	74	277,190	43,400	205	W	SH, built new
P-1aa	26x32	74	277,190	47,300	190	W	SH, from P-1
P-1b	26x28	74	299,000	44,600	205	W	SH, from P-1a
P-1ba	26x28	74	299,000	44,600	205	W	SH, from P-1 and P-1a
P-1c	26x28	74	299,000	44,600	205	W	SH, from various 2-8-2's
P-1ca	26x28	74	299,000	44,600	205	B	SH, from 2-8-2's
P-1d	26.5x28	74	318,500	51,000	225	W	SH, stokers, power reverse, large tenders
P-1da	26x28	74	311,000	48,900	225	W	SH, stokers, power reverse, large tenders

Valve Gear: "W" = Walschaerts, "B" = Baker
SH = superheated

Above: Class Q-4b Mikado 4476 (B&O referred to Mikados as "MacArthurs" after Gen. Douglas MacArthur, the World War II hero) and Class P-1aa Pacific 5076 take eastbound Train 30 out of Amblersburg, W.Va., in 1945. The railroad often double-headed a Mikado and a Pacific on the heavy grades in West Virginia. After diesels bumped the P-1 Pacifics off passenger runs, they could still be seen helping those trains over mountainous terrain.

Right: The photographer turns as the train passes to give us a better look at Pacific 5076. (both H.W. Pontin photos, Herbert H. Harwood Jr. Collection)

Class P-1d Pacific 5059 and Class P-1ba Pacific 5080 take Train 11, the westbound Metropolitan Special, out of Grafton, W.Va., on Aug. 15, 1947. The Pacifics are passing the old passenger station that was located between the old main line to Fairmont and the "Parkersburg Branch" that became the new main line when it opened in 1857. The building served other purposes until it was torn down a few years later. (Howard N. Barr Sr. photo, TLC Collection)

P-1d No. 5070 with Train 11, the Metropolitan Special, on the west end of the Cumberland Division, June 24, 1950 (William P. Price photo, TLC Collection)

Class P-1d Pacific 5057 – previously converted from Class P-1aa – stands ready to depart Kenova, W.Va., with Train 72 at 10:30 a.m. on May 12, 1949. The crew includes, from left, engineer Les Dyke, fireman John Lightner, flagman Bob Cariens and conductor John P. Hill. The 5057 was retired in 1955. (Bob Withers Collection)

Class P-1c Pacific 5008 rests between assignments at the coaling facility in Brunswick, Md., on Oct. 12, 1947. The 5008, which was converted from Class Q-1 Mikado 4137 in 1926, was sold for scrap in November 1953. (Max Miller photo, TLC Collection)

Class P-1c Pacific 5002 leaves Grafton, W.Va., with Train 65 for Connellsville, Pa., on Aug. 8, 1951. Two of the train's five cars are deadheading sleepers. The 5002, which was converted from Q-1 Mikado 4126 in 1926, was sold for scrap in November 1953. (E.L. Thompson photo, B&O Railroad Historical Society Collection)

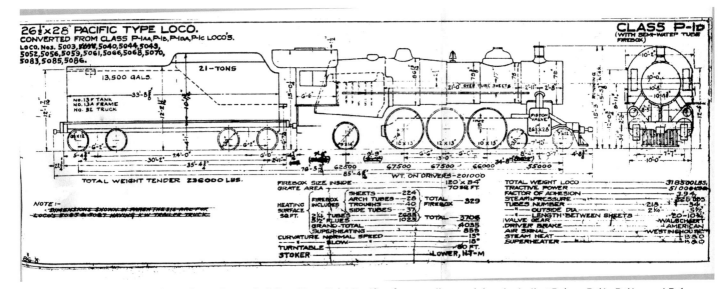

In 1928, Baltimore's Mount Clare Shops began building Class P-1d Pacifics from earlier models – including P-1aa, P-1b, P-1ba and P-1c. The P-1d class featured 26½x28 inch cylinders, 74-inch drivers, 318,500 pounds weight, 51,000 pounds tractive effort, and 225 pounds steam pressure. The P-1d class had large, square-tank tenders that carried 21 tons of coal and 13,500 gallons of water, Walschaerts valve gear, stokers and power reverse gears. Some had water scoops. The class was efficient, and comprised B&O's most powerful Pacific class. This B&O Railroad diagram shows the specs for engines equipped with semi-watertube fireboxes, including 5003, 5040, 5044, 5049, 5052, 5056, 5059, 5061, 5066, 5068, 5070, 5083, 5085 and 5086.

Class P-1d Pacific 5048 charges through Woodside, Md., just west of Silver Spring, with an eight-car Train 25, the westbound Fort Pitt Limited, at 1:47 p.m. March 13, 1932. The 5048 was originally a P-1c, having been converted from Class Q-1 Mikado 4048 in 1925. (Bruce D. Fales photo, Jay Williams Collection)

Class P-1d Pacific 5066 is seen at Magnolia, W.Va., with Train 22, the eastbound Cleveland-Baltimore Washingtonian, on Oct. 16, 1952. The straighter, faster Magnolia Cutoff goes across the original main line on a high bridge. The locomotive was scrapped in March 1954. (William P. Price photo, Bob Withers Collection)

Class P-1d Pacific 5003 charges through Patterson Creek, W.Va., on July 29, 1948, with an eastbound seven-car passenger train. (R.H. Kindig photo, TLC Collection)

Class P-1d Pacific 5003 takes Train 11, the westbound Metropolitan Special, out of Cumberland, Md., on Oct. 9, 1949. (William P. Price photo, Bob Withers Collection)

P-1d No. 5094 rolls east with a "Main Train" at Belden's Bend, W.Va. on October 15, 1946. (Bruce D. Fales photo, Jay Williams Collection)

Class P-1d Pacific 5043 forwards an eastbound four-car Train 30 around Salt Lick Curve near Terra Alta, W.Va., on Aug. 11, 1947. The locomotive, which was converted from Class Q-1 Mikado 4111 in 1924, was retired in 1956. (B&O Railroad Historical Society Collection)

P-1d Pacific No. 5087 with Train No. 9, the New York - Pittsburgh - Chicago Express, at Capitol View, Md., on March 23, 1944. (Bruce D. Fales photo, Jay Williams Collection)

Class P-1d Pacific 5070 loafs down Cranberry Grade at Amblersburg, W.Va., with Train 11, the westbound Metropolitan Special, in 1949. In those days and in that territory, No. 11 carried a Jersey City, N.J.-St. Louis sleeper, a dining/lounge car and individual-seat coaches. In later years, it would lose those amenities and gain a longer string of head-end cars, but at least it would survive until Amtrak's takeover in 1971. (Bert Penny-packer photo, Bob Withers Collection)

Same station, same train, another P-1d, and another date: Pacific 5086 chugs through Amblersburg with No. 11 in this undated view. This time, the passenger waiting shed is visible, which raises a question. Of the five westbound and six eastbound passenger trains listed in the Feb. 20, 1949, timetable, only eastbound Train 30 stopped here. We suppose Amblersburg passengers who boarded Train 30 had to hitchhike home. On second thought, that wouldn't work, either – no roads! (Bob's Photos, B&O Railroad Historical Society Collection)

Class P-1d Pacific 5085 coasts at 40 miles an hour down Cranberry Grade through Rodemer with an eight-car westbound Metropolitan Special. The 5085 began life as the 2170 in 1911 and was rebuilt seven years later. (R.H. Kindig photo, B&O Railroad Historical Society Collection)

Class P-1d Pacific 5036 takes Train 11, the westbound Metropolitan Special, down Cranberry Grade at Amblersburg, W.Va., on April 2, 1950. Baltimore's Mount Clare Shops rebuilt the engine as Class P-1c Pacific 5036 from a 2-8-2 in 1924 and it was reclassified as a P-1d six years later. It was taken out of service on Dec. 29, 1953. (B&O Railroad Historical Society Collection)

P-1d No. 5070 with a train at Hyndman, Pa., on July 27, 1947. (Charles A. Brown photo, TLC Collection)

P-1aa No. 5077 east of the station in Wheeling, W. Va., in October, 1948. The GM "Train of Tomorrow" is on display to the left. (J. J. Young photo, Bob Withers Collection)

P-1d No. 5094 is putting on a fine show of smoke at speed at CO Tower, McKenzie, Md. on April 6, 1947 (William P. Price photo, TLC Collection)

The fireman hoists his grip up to the deck of P-1d No. 5085 at Grafton, W. Va., on August 13, 1947. (Howard W. Ameling photo, Bob Withers Collection)

Class P-1d Pacific 5085 advances Train 11, the westbound Metropolitan Special, past K Tower at Blaser, W.Va., near the top of Cheat River Grade, on June 11. 1949. As soon as the train goes through Kingwood Tunnel, it will head down Newburg Grade toward Grafton. (W.H. Thrall photo, TLC Collection)

P-1d No. 5052 with a westbound mail-and-express train crossing the Potomac River at Harper's Ferry, W. Va., in April, 1948. (R. E. Tobey photo, H. H. Harwood Jr. Collection)

Class P-1d Pacific 5068 takes a nine-car troop train out of Grafton, W.Va., on the afternoon of Wednesday, May 20, 1953. Aboard its eight heavyweight sleepers and Army kitchen car are 202 Army draftees en route from Fort George G. Meade, Md., to 16 weeks of Infantry basic training at Camp Breckenridge, Ky. The signing of an armistice ending the Korean War barely two months later also will signal the end, for all practical purposes, of the troop train era. Note that No. 5068 has been equipped with a solid pilot, as were a few P-5s and P-6s as well. (Philip R. Hastings photo, Bob Withers Collection)

We see Class P-1d Pacific 5068 again, but not on such a glamorous mission. Engineer Glen Hardman has brought Grafton-Wheeling Train 343 into Fairmont, W.Va., at 6:25 on an August 1948 morning. Fireman C.A. Clark fills the locomotive's water tank during the station stop. (O.V. Nelson photo, Bob Withers Collection)

Class P-1d Pacific 5049 takes Train 11, the westbound Metropolitan Special, across the Tygart Valley River bridge at Grafton, W.Va., at 2:29 p.m. July 27, 1949. (Bruce D. Fales photo, Jay Williams Collection)

The P-3 Class Pacifics

Baldwin built 30 hand-fired Class P-3 Pacifics for B&O, numbered 5100-5129, between July and September in 1913. They came equipped with 24x28 inch cylinders, 76-inch drivers, Walschaerts valve gear and power reverse gears, weighed 248,600 pounds and developed 38,000 pounds of tractive effort and 210 pounds steam pressure.

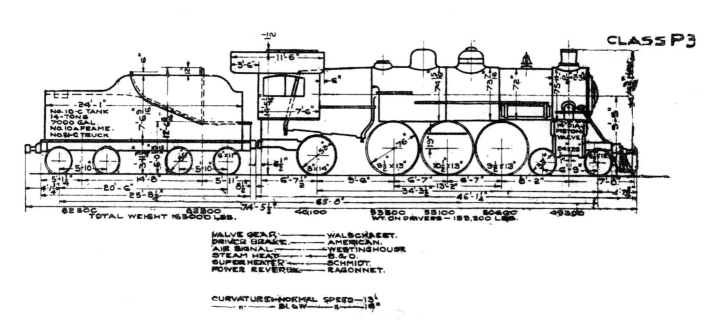

Class P-3 Roster		
Number	**Built**	**Retired**
5100	July, 1913	December-1948
5101	July, 1913	December-1951
5102	July, 1913	October-1951
5103	July, 1913	May-1952
5104	August, 1913	October-1947
5105	August, 1913	October-1949
5106	August, 1913	June-1951
5107	August, 1913	March-1951
5108	August, 1913	March-1951
5109	August, 1913	January-1953
5110	August, 1913	May-1952
5111	August, 1913	July-1950
5112	August, 1913	September-1950
5113	August, 1913	February-1951
5114	August, 1913	May-1951

Number	**Built**	**Retired**
5115	August, 1913	April-1948
5116	August, 1913	June-1950
5117	August, 1913	April-1951
5118	August, 1913	November-1950
5119	August, 1913	July-1950
5120	August, 1913	April-1946
5121	August, 1913	June-1951
5122	August, 1913	April-1952
5123	August, 1913	May-1952
5124	August, 1913	May-1950
5125	September, 1913	January-1953
5126	September, 1913	May-1952
5127	September, 1913	August-1951
5128	September, 1913	May-1952
5129	September, 1913	June-1952
All were built by the Baldwin Locomotive Works		

Opposite Top: B&O Railroad diagram sheet for the P-3 class.

Opposite Below: Baldwin Locomotive Works builder's photos of P-3 No. 5112. The lower images shows how the "dumping" tender's coal bunker would tip up and forward to move the coal closer to the fireman. (TLC Collection)

Class P-3 Pacific 5113 rests between assignments in Baltimore on May 9, 1948. Her original "dumping" tender has been replaced with a more conventional rectangular tender, taken from a D-30 class 0-6-0 switcher. Note the diesel switcher at right – a sign of the times. Because of increasing dieselization, the 35-year-old 5113 would live less than another three years. (Howard Ameling photo, Bob Withers Collection)

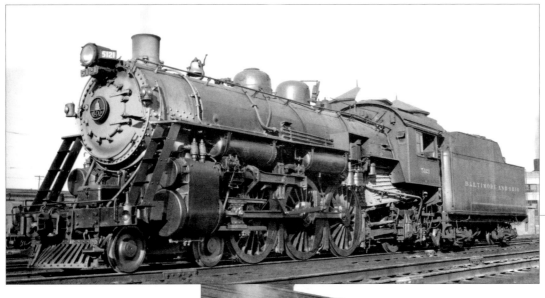

With attractively proportioned lines and a clean smokebox, Class P-3 Pacific 5121 rests between assignments at Washington, D.C., on March 21, 1940. (TLC Collection)

Class P-3 Pacific 5129, the last of its class, lets off a little steam near the roundhouse at the Ivy City engine terminal in Washington, D.C., on Sept. 13, 1946. Note that this engine is equipped with a pair of single cylinder air compressors under the running board just in front of the fire box, while No. 5121, above, is equipped with the newer cross-compound air compressor. (L.W. Rice photo, TLC Collection)

Class P-3 Pacific 5107 departs Connellsville, Pa., with a four-car Train 66 for Grafton, W.Va., at 11 a.m. on Saturday, Sept. 3, 1949. The little train may not look like much, but at the time it boasted a reclining-seat coach with a lunch counter and lounge rooms to make the 92.5-mile, three-hour 40-minute trip more enjoyable. The locomotive said farewell to the world in March 1951; the train lasted until 1953. (John F. Humiston photo, TLC Collection)

Opposite: Class P-3 5100, first of its class, has forwarded 12 PRR cars full of Weirton (W.Va.) High School football players and fans from Wheeling, W.Va., to Parkersburg. W.Va., for a football game in 1934. The train has unloaded its passengers at Parkersburg's Ann Street Station (out of sight to the left) and the photographer is standing on the elevated platform to catch a shot after the train has backed up into the Low Yard and is heading around the transfer track to the High Yard. While the locomotive is serviced at the roundhouse, the train will be taken across the Ohio River to Belpre, Ohio, for turning on a wye. (Stephen P. Davidson photo, Bob Withers Collection)

According to the photographer, it's 10 a.m. on Friday, June 6, 1947, and in exactly one hour Class P-3 Pacific 5112 will forward Train 72 from Kenova, W.Va., toward Parkersburg, Wheeling and Pittsburgh. We suspect that the photographer erred slightly with the date. The train has only its 30-foot RPO apartment car, a coach, and no express car. The express car did not run on Sundays, so we offer a theory that the photo was made on Sunday, June 8. (Leo Harmon photo, Bob Withers Collection)

Class P-3 Pacific 5126 stands with a passenger train at North Vernon, Ind., on May 8, 1934. At the time, all B&O passenger service was still in steam, so the P-3 could have been in the middle of a run between Cincinnati Union Terminal and Shops (one mile west of Washington, Ind.) or handling a train operating between North Vernon and Louisville. (R.W. Legg photo, Jay Williams Collection)

The P-4 Class Pacifics

Baldwin built 10 Class P-4 Pacifics for B&O, numbered 5130-5139, between August 1917 and February 1918. They were identical to the P-3 Class, except that they weighed 255,500 pounds and had Vanderbilt tenders. One of them, the 5131, was retired in 1937, and the final two, the 5132 and the 5138, were sold for scrap in January 1953.

P-4 Roster		
Number	**Built**	**Retired**
5130	August, 1917	September, 1952
5131	August, 1917	1937
5132	August, 1917	January, 1953
5133	September, 1917	May, 1951
5134	September, 1917	January, 1952
5135	November, 1917	October, 1952
5136	December, 1917	December, 1952
5137	January, 1918	December, 1952
5138	January, 1918	January, 1953
5139	February, 1918	December, 1951
All were built by the Baldwin Locomotive Works		

B&O Railroad diagram of the P-4 Pacific

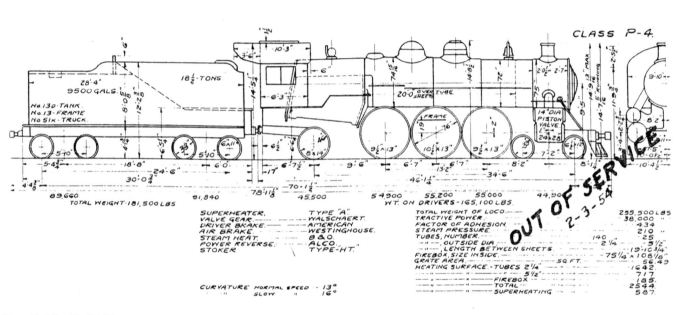

Class P-4 Pacific 5137 gets some much-needed attention beside the coal dock in Parkersburg, W.Va.,'s High Yard in October 1950. (Stephen P. Davidson photo, Jay Williams Collection)

Above: Class P-4 Pacific 5137 charges through a January 1950 snowstorm between Benwood and Wheeling, W.Va., on the last lap of an early morning trip with Train 430 from Grafton. At the time, the train carried a reclining-seat coach with lunch counter and lounge rooms and a 10-section/2-compartment/1-drawing room sleeper from Jersey City, N.J., having been forwarded on Train 509 to Washington, D.C., and Train 23 to Grafton. Because of a timetable quirk, the train ran as westbound No. 343 from Grafton to Moundsville, W.Va., on the Monongah Division and as eastbound No. 430 from Moundsville to Wheeling on the Wheeling Division. Incidentally, the snow kept falling until there was 39 inches on the ground. Retired railroaders still talk today about how many days they were stranded somewhere before they got home. (J.J. Young Jr. photo, Bob Withers Collection)

Opposite Top: Class P-4 Pacific 5133 blasts its way out of No. 23 Tunnel, located 0.8 mile east of Kanawha Station between Clarksburg and Parkersburg, W.Va., on the Monongah Division with a local passenger train in this undated photo. The tunnel was daylighted during World War II. (Dr. H.R. Blackburn photo, Jay Williams Collection)

Opposite Below: Class P-4 Pacific 5136 stands at Decatur, Ill., on May 4, 1949, with what appears to be Train 49, due out at 7:30 a.m. for Indianapolis. The two-car train appears to have a baggage/mail car with a 15-foot RPO compartment and a single straight-back-seat coach. What are the Indianapolis passengers going to eat during their four-hour, 15-minute journey? (Bruce D. Fales photo, Jay Williams Collection)

The P-5 Class Pacifics

During World War I, the United States Railroad Administration hired mechanical engineers from several railroads to design standard steam locomotive types to expedite the construction of much-needed power for the overburdened carriers and to equip the engines with standardized parts to enable one railroad to transfer them to another carrier to fill emergency needs without having to transport parts for maintenance and repairs. The idea also was economical for the builders.

B&O received 30 "light" USRA Pacifics in 1918-1919, placing them in the P-5 class. Baldwin built Nos. 5200-5219 and Alco built Nos. 5220-5229. They came equipped with Baker valve gear, 25x28 inch cylinders, 73-inch drivers, 200 pounds steam pressure, power reverse gears, grate shakers, coal pushers and superheaters. They weighed 288,000 pounds and developed 40,200 pounds tractive effort.

In the early 1920s, the railroad increased the size of the drivers to 74". Mount Clare added front-delivery stokers in 1940. Walschaerts valve gear replaced the Baker gear on 20 of the locomotives, and they were reclassified as P-5a. All of the class eventually received new fireboxes, raising tractive effort to 42,200 pounds and steam pressure to 210 pounds.

The P-5 locomotives began their lives as the principal passenger power between Washington, D.C., and Philadelphia. Seven years later, they were the first locomotive group to run through between Washington, Philadelphia and Jersey City via B&O, Reading and Jersey Central after the Pennsylvania Railroad finally revoked its World War I permission for B&O trains to go directly into New York City's Penn Station on Aug. 29, 1926.

Their tenders originally held 14 tons of coal and 10,000 gallons of water, but in 1926 some of those tenders were extended by 9 feet so they could carry 18 tons of coal and 14,500 gallons of water. The reason? A scarcity of track pans on the "Royal Blue Line" – pans that were placed there in the first place to speed up the watering process and help B&O trains better compete with PRR's racehorses. The downside was that now the locomotives required 90-foot turntables, whereas they once had needed only 80 feet. The long distances between water pans convinced B&O to doublehead trains of 10 or more cars - not to speed them up but to keep from working the engines hard so they would conserve water.

P-5 Roster		
Number	*Built*	*Retired*
5200	June, 1919	October, 1956
5201	June, 1919	July, 1954
5202	June, 1919	June, 1954
5203	June, 1919	April, 1954
5204	June, 1919	October, 1956
5205	June, 1919	July, 1954
5206	June, 1919	October, 1956
5207	June, 1919	September, 1953
5208	June, 1919	January, 1954
5209	June, 1919	January, 1954
5210	June, 1919	October, 1953
5211	June, 1919	May, 1953
5212	June, 1919	October, 1956
5213	July, 1919	December, 1953
5214	July, 1919	April, 1954
5215	July, 1919	July, 1955
5216	July, 1919	April, 1955
5217	July, 1919	January, 1955
5218	July, 1919	October, 1956
5219	August, 1919	August, 1956
5220	September, 1919	October, 1956
5221	September, 1919	October, 1956
5222	September, 1919	October, 1956
5223	September, 1919	October, 1956
5224	September, 1919	1955
5225	September, 1919	December, 1953
5226	September, 1919	July, 1954
5227	September, 1919	July, 1955
5228	September, 1919	January, 1955
5229	September, 1919	January, 1954

Nos. 5200 – 5219 were built by the Baldwin Locomotive Works.

Nos. 5220 – 5229 were built by the Brooks Works of the American Locomotive Company.

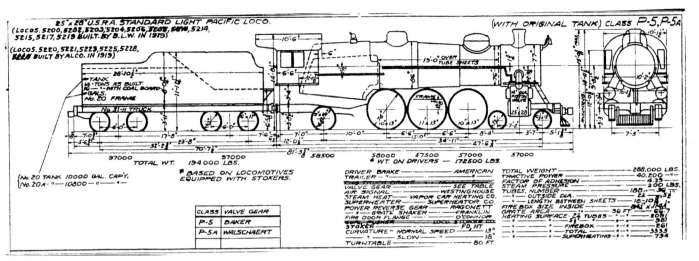

B&O Railroad diagram of the P-5 class locomotive.

Baldwin Locomotive Works builder's photo of P-5 No. 5204. Baldwin built the first 20 of the 30 P-5 locomotives, built to the design of the USRA light Pacific. Both of the photos on this page show the original USRA configuration of appliances, including the bell at the top of the smokebox front, headlight centered on the smokebox front, coal pushers in the tender, and Commonwealth tender trucks. (TLC Collection)

American Locomotive Company (Alco) builder's photo of P-5 No. 5224. Alco built the last 10 of the 30 P-5 locomotives. (TLC Collection)

Opposite Top: A work crew inspects Class P-5 Pacific 5222, minus its tender and cylinder head cover, on the turntable in Washington, Ind., in March 1931. Note the ladder on the pilot deck. (TLC Collection)

Opposite Below: Class P-5a Pacific 5208 backs past the Ivy City coach yard to pick up a train in the Washington, D.C., Union Station at 10:30 a.m. on Dec. 7, 1931. Beginning in the early 1930s, the B&O began modifying the P-5s to match the styling of other locomotives. The bell is now on the top of the boiler between the sandbox and steam dome, the headlight is at the top of the smokebox front, and the tender is equipped with Andrews trucks. When the 5208 receives a stoker, the coal pusher will be removed from the tender. (Bruce D. Fales photo, Jay Williams Collection)

Class P-5a Pacific 5227 rests over an inspection pit in Baltimore's Riverside Yard in 1937. From the looks of the smokebox emblem, the locomotive will be taking the next Capitol Limited out of town. (B&O photo, TLC Collection)

P-5a No. 5201 leaving the Michigan Central Station in Detroit, Michigan, on April 2, 1949, displays her enlarged tender, rebuilt from her original USRA tender. The railroad increased the size of the coal bunker by building it higher, and increased the water capacity by lengthening the tank by 10 feet. The seam where the back wall of the tank was originally located is clearly visible between the "H" and "I" in "OHIO". (Elmer Treloar photo, TLC Collection)

Class P-5a Pacific 5214 escorts Train 1, the westbound National Limited, across the Pennsylvania Railroad's "Panhandle Line" diamond at Relay Depot in East St. Louis, Ill., at 1 p.m. on Sept. 15, 1937. The Mississippi River, St. Louis Union Station, and the end of the crew's work day are just ahead. Note that the smokebox front on this engine has been reworked and now sports only the 12 door lugs commonly used on the B&O. Easily visible here are the conical sandbox lids, a common feature on B&O's USRA Pacifics and Mikados. (Bruce D. Fales photo, Jay Williams Collection)

This is the same train, the westbound National Limited, only two days later and a little closer to the station at 1:11 p.m. This time, Class P-5a Pacific 5227 is doing the honors. To the left of the locomotive is the former Royal Blue lightweight train set, now in use on the B&O controlled Alton RR on the Abe Lincoln and Ann Rutledge trains. (Bruce D. Fales photo, Jay Williams Collection)

Class P-5a Pacific 5214 rests between assignments at the East St. Louis, Ill., engine facility in 1938. Notice that the tender has been extended by 9 feet, evidence that the locomotive was assigned to the Washington, D.C.,-Jersey City, N.J., Royal Blue Line and its scarce track pans before the P-7 class came in 1927. (Bruce D. Fales photo, Jay Williams Collection)

Class P-5a Pacific 5215 is about to depart the Philadelphia station at 24th and Chestnut streets with 10 cars in 1939. The shiny locomotive looks like it's just out of the bathtub. (B&O photo, TLC Collection)

Class P-5a Pacific 5203 takes mail and express Train 29 across Spooky Hollow Trestle between Loveland and Madeira, Ohio, in the mid-1940s. The engine's original length tender is evidence that not all P-5s' tenders were lengthened. (Dan Finfrock Collection)

A hostler is moving Class P-5a Pacific 5216 to the next spot for servicing at Pere Marquette's engine terminal in Detroit on April 2, 1950. It looks like this locomotive's tender had been extended, too. Rarely for this class, the smokebox on this engine has been lagged (insulation and a jacket applied.) (Bruce D. Fales photo, Jay Williams Collection)

Class P-5a Pacific 5224 crosses over to another main line at Halethorpe, Md., with a string of passenger equipment from Great Britain's Londonderry, Seaham & Sunderland Railway on May 24, 1943. The equipment had been on display at the 1939 New York World's Fair and was being held over in Baltimore until World War II was over. Note that a round B&O Capitol Dome emblem has replaced the round number plate at the center of the smokebox, and that this engine retains the flat sandbox covers it was delivered with. (B&O photo, Joe Schmitz Collection)

Class P-5a Pacific 5210 charges out of Detroit with an eight-car Train 53, the Great Lakes Limited, *on April 28, 1946. It was the first B&O train to depart from the Michigan Central terminal. (TLC Collection)*

Class P-5a Pacific 5218 heads for the engine servicing facilities across the Mississippi River in Illinois after delivering a train to St. Louis Union Station in 1950. Note the incoming Missouri Pacific train in front of Tower No. 1. (B&O Railroad photo, TLC Collection)

Class P-5a Pacific 5229 charges toward RS&G Junction – the point at which the Ohio River line connects with the Ravenswood, Spencer & Glenville branch – after departing Ravenswood, W.Va., with Train 73 on Oct. 23, 1951. Obviously, environmental concerns are far in the future as an inexperienced fireman makes plenty of black smoke to coat sheets hanging on local clotheslines with soot. (Richard J. Cook photo, Bob Withers Collection)

Class P-5a Pacific 5213 brings Wheeling-Kenova, W.Va., Train 73 into Parkersburg, W.Va.'s, Ann Street Station in the early 1950s. The station's elevated platform seems short on passengers, doesn't it? Few people are aware of it, but this locomotive took the first westbound run of the five-car all-Pullman out of Baltimore on May 13, 1923. Standing on the open rear platform of the observation car between Mount Royal and Camden stations was none other than B&O President Daniel Willard, an indication of the train's importance to the company. Alas, the carrier's respect did not extend to the "first locomotive." Here it is on a nondescript local passenger run, and it will be sold for scrap in December 1953. (Artcraft Studio photo, Bob Withers Collection)

The company finally had its way with the West Virginia Public Service Commission, and Train 77 arrived in Kenova for the final time on Sunday morning, Sept. 27, 1953. So here, east of Guyandotte (East Huntington) on Sunday afternoon, Class P-5a Pacific 5229 and Class P-5 Pacific 5209 doublehead an enlarged Train 72 toward Wheeling with mostly deadheading equipment. (Charles Lemley photo, Bob Withers Collection)

Class P-5a Pacific 5224 pauses at Lima, Ohio, with Cincinnati-Toledo all-stops local Train 356 in July or August 1953. Note the twin sealed beam headlight, installed by the B&O on many locomotives in the early 1950s as a safety measure, ensuring that even if a bulb burns out, the second one will still provide light. (Herbert H. Harwood Jr. photo, TLC Collection)

Class P-5 Pacific 5209 stands at Kenova, W.Va., on Nov. 6, 1951, with a four-car Train 78 (baggage car 660, 30-foot apartment RPO 227, coach 5205 and 12-section/drawing room sleeper McElrath) that will depart that night. Sadly, the photo was made to present as evidence for the company's first application to the PSC to have the train discontinued. The sleeper fared better than the rest of the equipment in subsequent years – the locomotive was sold for scrap in January 1954; we assume the head-end cars and coach also eventually met the torch; but the author spotted the McElrath (painted red and disguised as camp car X4523) sitting on blocks and serving as a yard office in Cincinnati in the summer of 1968. (Charles Lemley photo, Bob Withers Collection)

Class P-5a Pacific 5220 stands on Track 2, ready in 1956 to take Train 73 out of Wheeling, W.Va., after Class P-7c Pacific 5305 leaves with Train 233 for Cincinnati. The 5220 will have an easy time of it, hauling only an express car and coach to Kenova. (TLC Collection)

Class P-5a Pacific 5220 pauses at Huntington, W.Va., with Train 73 in May 1956. It looks like a couple of people are waiting to pick up a loved one who has come in on the train. The locomotive is just five months away from retirement; the train will last until Jan. 31, 1957. (Herbert H. Harwood Jr. photo, Bob Withers Collection)

THE P-6 CLASS PACIFICS

Baldwin built 15 Class P-6 Pacifics for B&O in 1922. These locomotives weighed 288,600 pounds and developed 40,200 pounds of tractive effort and 200 pounds steam pressure. They came equipped with 25x28 inch cylinders, 74-inch drivers, hand-screw reverse gears, coal pushers and Vanderbilt tenders, but no stokers. They were also equipped with cast steel trailing trucks that could be fitted with boosters, although the B&O never chose to do so.

Prior to 1927, the P-6 engines handled passenger trains between Cumberland, Md., Washington, D.C., and Philadelphia, with Reading Company Pacifics taking over between Philadelphia and Jersey City, N.J.

By 1932, Walschaert valve gear replaced the locomotives' original Baker valve gear and the steam pressure was raised to 210 pounds, and they were reclassified as P-6a. Three of them were assigned new numbers on Nov. 1, 1956, although it is possible the 5231 and the 5241 never received them before all three were taken out of service in 1957. The author spotted the 151 (former 5237) on a weed-spraying work train in Huntington, W.Va., on May 20-21, 1957, and the 5231, still sporting its old number, on mixed Train 81 into Kenova on Saturday, May 25, 1957, and double-heading back to Parkersburg that evening with Q-3 MacArthur 395 (former 4598) on freight Train 92.

P-6 Roster			
Number	Renumbered 1957	Built	Retired
5230		October, 1922	1955
5231	150	October, 1922	1957
5232		December, 1922	1956
5233		December, 1922	June, 1951
5234		December, 1922	June, 1951
5235		December, 1922	June, 1951
5236		December, 1922	1955
5237	151	December, 1922	1957
5238		December, 1922	1956
5239		December, 1922	1956
5240		December, 1922	June, 1954
5241	152	December, 1922	1957
5242		December, 1922	1955
5243		December, 1922	1955
5244		December, 1922	1956

All were built by the Baldwin Locomotive Works.

All were reclassified to P-6a, with Walschaerts valve gear replacing the original Baker valve gear, and the steam pressure raised to 210 psi, by 1932.

Class EL-1a 2-8-8-0 7113 is in the clear at Echo, Pa., as P-6a Pacific 5232 charges past with coach-only Buffalo, N.Y.-Pittsburgh, Pa., Train 251 in 1954. Baldwin built the 5232 in December 1922 and the engine was retired in 1956. P-6s were the standard locomotive in the last days of passenger service on the Buffalo Division, replacing ex BR&P P-17s and P-18s. (G.C. Corey photo, Herbert H. Harwood Jr. Collection)

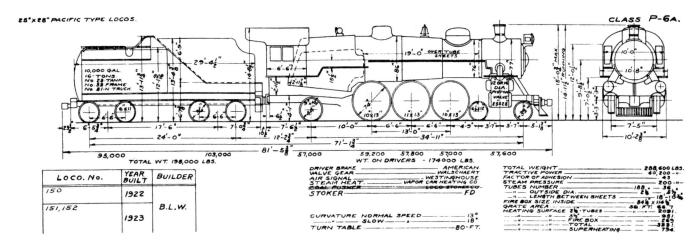

25"×28" PACIFIC TYPE LOCOS. — CLASS P-6A.

10,000 GAL.
16 TONS.
No. 23 TANK
No. 33 FRAME
No. 81-H TRUCK

TOTAL WT. 198,000 LBS.

WT. ON DRIVERS - 174,000 LBS.

LOCO. No.	YEAR BUILT	BUILDER
150	1922	
151,152	1923	B.L.W.

DRIVER BRAKE ———————— AMERICAN
VALVE GEAR ———————— WALSCHAERT
AIR SIGNAL ———————— WESTINGHOUSE
STEAM HEAT. ———————— VAPOR CAR HEATING CO.
COAL PUSHER ———————— LOCO STOKER CO.
STOKER ———————— FD

CURVATURE NORMAL SPEED ———— 13°
      " SLOW " ———— 18°
TURN TABLE ———————— 80-FT.

TOTAL WEIGHT ———————— 288,600 LBS.
TRACTIVE POWER ———————— 40,200 "
FACTOR OF ADHESION ———————— 4.3
STEAM PRESSURE ———————— 200-#
TUBES NUMBER ———— 188 " 36
    " OUTSIDE DIA. ———— 2¼ " 5½
    " LENGTH BETWEEN SHEETS ———— 18'-0"
FIRE BOX SIZE INSIDE ———— 84⅛ X 114¾
GRATE AREA ———— 58 SQ. FT.
HEATING SURFACE 2¼-TUBES ———— 2091
    " 5½ " ———— 351
    " FIRE BOX ———— 269
    " TOTAL ———— 3331
    " SUPERHEATING ———— 734

50

Above: Even in their younger days, the Class P-6a Pacifics sometimes were assigned to haul freight. Here, locomotive 5243 has a westbound local in tow at Garrett, Ind., circa 1936. Not fitted with a power reverse, the linkage from the valve gear to the Johnson Bar in the cab is very prominent under the running board. The U.S. 27 crossing later was later routed under the tracks through an underpass. The 5243 was retired in 1955. (Jay Williams Collection)

Opposite Top: B&O Railroad diagram of the P-6a class. Note that this is a late diagram, in that is shows the engines with the numbers assigned in 1956. Note too that it indicates that the coal pusher has been removed and the locomotive has been fitted with a B&O design front delivery stoker.

Opposite Center: P-6a No. 5240 is seen here with a second Pacific on the head end of the westbound Fort Pitt Limited taking water at Garrett, Ind. on July 16, 1933. (Robert B. Graham photo, Jay Williams collection)

Opposite Bottom: No. 5240 appears again, this time from the other side, again doubleheaded with another Pacific, this time in 1950. By now 5240 has been fitted with over-fire jets to reduce production of black smoke, and its smokebox has been lagged. (Jay Williams collection)

Right: Part of Train 72's crew – engineer M.J. "Daddy" Reed, left, and conductor Herbert W. Sammons – pose with P-6a Pacific 5244 in Huntington, W.Va., on Jan. 31, 1957. Pass riders wanting to take the last trip of this train have virtually filled the coach. That's Bea Lawwill, a clerk in Huntington's district freight office, temporarily keeping the engineer's seat warm. (Charles Lemley photo, Bob Withers Collection)

Class P-6a 5241 and another Pacific charge eastward out of Garrett, Ind., with Train 8, the eastbound Fort Pitt Limited. In 1934, Train 8 out of Chicago carried sleepers for Wheeling (via Train 46 from Willard, Ohio), Pittsburgh, Washington and Jersey City, N.J., in addition to coaches and a lounge car. Train 8 would pick up a diner in Akron, Ohio, and a parlor car in Pittsburgh. (Robert Graham photo, Jay Williams Collection)

Class P-6a Pacific 5241 leaves Utica, Ohio, just after sunrise – 6:28 a.m. if it's on time – on July 22, 1956, with Chicago-Wheeling, W.Va., Train 246. The train is carrying a reclining-seat coach, diner/lounge and 8-section/4-double-bedroom sleeper. Notice that the engine, which will be retired the following year, now has lost its Vanderbilt tender. (John A. Rehor photo, TLC Collection)

Class P-6a 5244 sits on the elevated tracks at Wheeling, W.Va., in April 1952 with Kenova-bound Train 73 as Train 233 leaves for Cincinnati. In 1952, Wheeling still hosted trains to and from from Pittsburgh, Grafton, Kenova, Cincinnati and Chicago. The power reverse is prominent under the running board ahead of the firebox. (J.J. Young Jr. photo, Bob Withers Collection)

Some of the P-6a class of Pacifics plied their last miles on the Wheeling Division. Here, at the Wheeling, W.Va., station in April 1949, the 5244 waits on Track 1 with Train 73 for Kenova until the 5238 departs from Track 2 with Pittsburgh-Cincinnati Train 33. While we wait, Baldwin yard switcher 449 (later 9236) rumbles past on Track 3 with a mine run for the Valley Camp Mine in Elm Grove, W.Va. (J.J. Young Jr. photo, Bob Withers Collection)

Class P-6a Pacific 5231 stops at the station at Moundsville, W.Va., on a raw winter day in 1955 or '56. Train 73, which is living on borrowed time, carries only an express car and coach, having lost its 30-foot apartment RPO car on Sept. 1, 1955. The locomotive has a larger tender from a retired P-1d, allowing it to travel farther between water stops. About 15 years later, the tidy little station will figure prominently in the James Stewart movie "Fool's Parade." (J.J. Young Jr. photo, Bob Withers Collection)

Class P-6a Pacific 5237 pauses at Williamstown, W.Va., with Wheeling-Kenova Train 73 on Dec. 23, 1954. It looks like the fireman is waiting for a hand signal to leave. (F.W. Schneider photo, TLC Collection)

Class P-6a Pacific 5231 rests between assignments at the roundhouse in the High Yard (Baltimore-St. Louis main line) at Parkersburg, W.Va., in August 1954. Chances are, the locomotive is being used on Wheeling-Kenova Trains 72 and 73, which pass through Parkersburg's Low Yard. (Bob Withers Collection)

Class P-6a Pacific 5237 is sitting in the tiny engine terminal in Kenova, W.Va., on April 23, 1956. It will depart on the next Train 72 for Parkersburg and Wheeling. (W.E. Hopkins photo, Bob Withers Collection)

Class P-6a Pacific 5244 departs Kenova with Train 72 in February 1956. The tiny B&O combination station is hidden behind the coach, but clearly visible is the elevated Norfolk & Western mainline and N&W / C&O Union Station just down the road. (Herbert H. Harwood Jr. photo, Bob Withers Collection)

Class P-6a Pacific 5231 brings Train 73 into Parkersburg, W.Va.'s ornate Ann Street Station for the last time on Jan. 31, 1957. An extra coach has been added to the train to accommodate all the pass riders wanting to take the final trip. Once the train reaches Kenova, it will return immediately to Parkersburg, leaving only mixed Trains 81 and 82 running between Parkersburg and Kenova. Ann Street's ticket office has been closed for more than two years; everyone board-ing now must pay cash fares to the conductor. The station has two more years to exist before it is razed and its bricks used to pave Parkersburg streets. (Artcraft Studio photo, Bob Withers Collection)

Opposite: Let's not leave the P-6a's on such a sad note. Here, engine 5238 rests in Cincinnati on April 9, 1949. Its next trip could take it to Washington, Ind., Toledo, Ohio, or Chillicothe, Ohio. (Tommy Smart photo, Bob Withers Collection)

The P-7 and P-9 Class Pacifics

B&O was exactly 100 years old in 1927 when it took delivery of 20 Class P-7 Pacifics – Nos. 5300-5319 – from Baldwin. They were known as the "President Engines" because they displayed the names of 20 of the first 21 U.S. Presidents (you couldn't have two engines named President Adams, after all) on their cab sides. They were painted in Pullman green with lettering and striping in gold; the gold stripes were bordered with a hair-line maroon stripe on the locomotives and tenders. The engines weighed 326,000 pounds and came equipped with 27x28-inch cylinders, 80-inch drivers, Du Pont-Simplex stokers, type A superheaters, power reverse, Walschaerts valve gear, train control, water scoops, 230 pounds steam pressure and 50,000 pounds of tractive effort – more than any other Pacific up to that time. One of the locomotives received a booster on the rear truck, and all of the locomotives were designed to accommodate them.

The P-7 class immediately displaced the P-5 class as the locomotive of choice on the Royal Blue Line – in fact, they were designed specifically for the Washington-Jersey City corridor with tenders holding 17.5 tons of coal and 11,000 gallons of water.

Using a Mikado boiler, Mount Clare Shops built a similar locomotive, the 5320 *President Cleveland*, class P-9, in 1928. It was equipped with Caprotti poppet valve gear, an Emerson water-tube firebox, superheater, stoker, water-bottom tank, and a screw reverse gear. The air compressor was located between the frames, behind the drivers, and the headlight generator was positioned on the left side of the rear deck, convenient for adjustment from the ground. Piping, as far as possible, was suspend-ed from the running boards and welded together to eliminate screw joints. The exhaust steam pipe to the Elesco exhaust steam injector was located between the frames and was carried through the ash pan at the rear of the locomotive. Throngs of people enjoyed seeing the 5320's smooth lines at an exhibit in Atlantic City, N.J., soon after it was built.

The 5320's Caprotti poppet valve gear wasn't successful, however, and in 1929 it was re-placed by 27½x28-inch cylinders, 12-inch piston valves and Walschaert valve gear, raising tractive effort to 51,750 pounds and the class to P-9a. Then, in 1945, a P-7 boiler replaced the Emerson boiler and the 5320 reverted to the P-7 class.

The company tinkered with these engines, too, creating several subclasses – and modernized seven of them (5305, 5308, 5309, 5312, 5314, 5317 and 5318) between 1944 and 1949. Classed P-7c, the modernized locomotives – painted solid blue with no striping nor presidential names, as were all P-7s – now boasted solid cast-steel beds, in which the frame, cross braces, cylinders, pilot deck and pump brackets are all one casting. They were given feed-water heaters, smokebox throttles, larger tenders, and air pumps and after-cooler pipes hidden behind a shield on the pilot that carrying the B&O Capitol Dome emblem. Headlights were repositioned in the center of the smokebox doors with bells placed above them, and classification lamps raised higher. All of which gave the locomotives a huskier appearance of speed and power.

The 5306 was transferred to Class P-7b in 1942 when it received a company-designed Type R superheater with a special plate on top of the smokebox. The 5304 became a P-7a when it was modified and streamlined in 1937 for the Royal Blue. Its

Baldwin Locomotive Works builder's photo of P-7 No. 5300, President Washington. *(TLC Collection)*

tender held 19.5 tons of coal and 13,000 gallons of water. But the 5304 lost its shroud two years later and reverted to Class P-7. Ironically, the 5304 became the only B&O engine to be streamlined twice when it joined the 5301, 5302 and 5303 in Class P-7d when the four of them were streamlined in 1946 for the Baltimore-Cincinnati *Cincinnatian*.

The company – in an effort to compete with the Chesapeake & Ohio's planned-but-eventually-canceled *Chessie* and the Norfolk & Western's *Powhatan Arrow* in the East Coast-Cincinnati daylight market – arranged a speedy 12½-hour all-day schedule for the B&O's 570-mile route, limiting the train to five rebuilt cars and prohibiting stops to add helpers in the mountains. Sadly, after 3½ years, declining ridership on the Baltimore-Cincinnati route, caused the train to be moved to a Cincinnati-Detroit route.

The *Cincinnatian's* locomotive tenders held 25 tons of coal and 20,000 gallons of water, ensuring 90 miles of travel between water stops. Since the engines were changed in each direction at Grafton, W.Va., they could leave that point with full loads of coal and water, taking additional water only at a few stations such as Martinsburg, W.Va., and Athens, Ohio. Their scoops were removed because there were no water pans on the route.

Between 1944 and 1953, six P-7 engines – 5312, 5314, 5315, 5316, 5317, and 5319 – were modernized like their P-7c sisters, but were classified as P-7e because they were equipped with roller bearings and tenders with six-wheel trucks and a capacity of 25 tons of coal and 20,000 gallons of water. The 5310 was reclassified a P-9a in 1939 when it received a water-tube firebox, but reverted to P-7a when that firebox and its boiler were traded out in 1947.

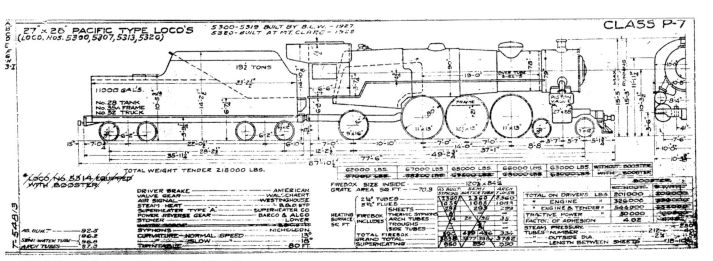

B&O Railroad diagram of the class P-7 Pacific.

B&O Railroad diagram of the class P-7a Pacific, streamlined for service on the Royal Blue between Washington, D.C., and Jersey City, N.J. The streamlined covering was removed in 1939 and the locomotive reverted to class P-7.

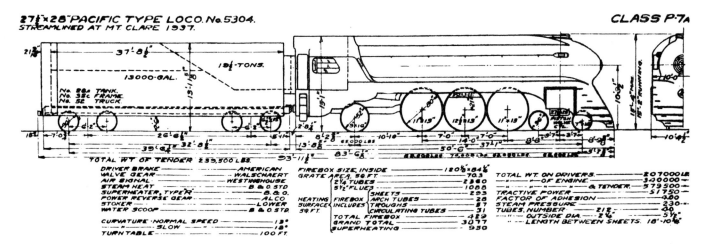

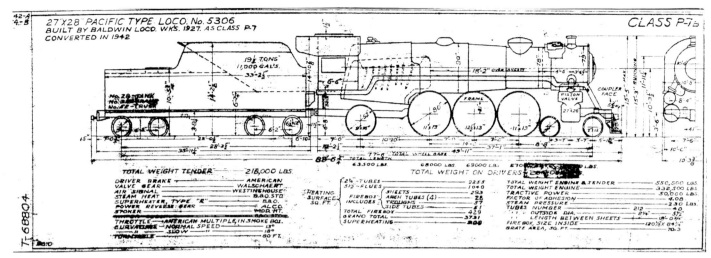

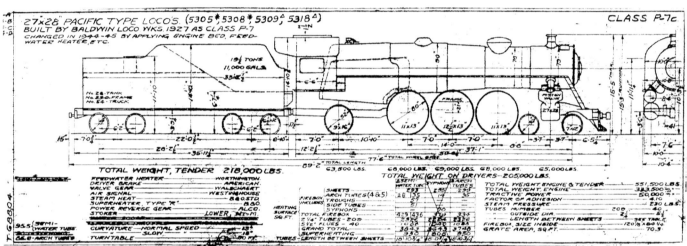

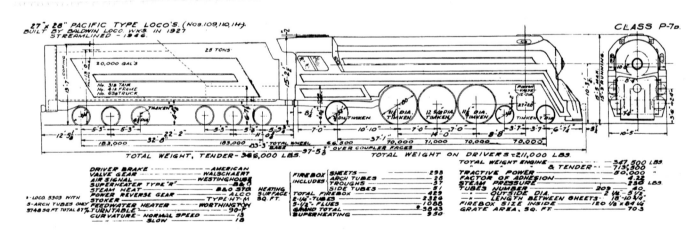

B&O Railroad diagrams for class P-7b, P-7c, and P-7d Pacifics.

P-7 Subclass Differences Summary from P-7	
P-7a	streamlined for *Royal Blue*, tender 18.5 T, 13,000 gal
P-7b	company designed Type R superheater with front end throttle
P-7c	cast engine bed, feed water heater, Type R superheater with front end throttle, air pumps and after-coolers on pilot deck, larger tender
P-7d	streamlined for *The Cincinnatian*, equipped with roller bearings on all axles, including tender, same mechanical improvements as the P-7c, tender 25T, 20,000 gal
P-7e	like P-7c but with roller bearings, tender 25T, 20,000 gal

			P-7 and P-9 Roster		
Number	**2nd Number**	**Built**	**Rebuilt to Class**	**Retired**	**Presidential Name**
5300	100	Feb-27		1957	Washington
5301	109	Feb-27	P-7d	1957	Adams
5302		Feb-27	P-7d	1956	Jefferson
5303	110	Feb-27	P-7d	1957	Madison
5304	111	Feb-27	P-7a, P-7, P-7d	1957	Monroe
5305	105	Apr-27	P-7c	1957	Jackson
5306	104	Apr-27	P-7b	1957	Van Buren
5307	101	Apr-27		1957	Harrison
5308	106	Apr-27	P-7c	1957	Tyler
5309	107	Apr-27	P-7c w/ booster	1957	Polk
5310	103	Apr-27	P-9b, P-7a	1957	Taylor
5311		Apr-27		Oct-53	Fillmore
5312	112	Apr-27	P-7c, P-7e	1957	Pierce
5313	102	Apr-27		1957	Buchanon
5314	113	Apr-27	P-7c w/ booster, P-7e	1957	Lincoln
5315		Apr-27	P-7e	1956	Johnson
5316	114	Apr-27	P-7e	1957	Grant
5317	115	Apr-27	P-7c	1957	Hayes
5318	108	Apr-27	P-7c	1957	Garfield
5319	116	Apr-27	P-7e	1957	Arthur
5320		May-28	P-9a, P-7	1956	Cleveland

Nos. 5300 – 5319 are class P-7, built by the Baldwin Locomotive Works.

No. 5320 is class P-9, built by the B&O Mt. Clare Shops.

P-7 No. 5300, *President Washington,* is preserved at the B&O Railroad Museum in Baltimore, Md.

B&O Railroad diagram for P-7e Pacific.

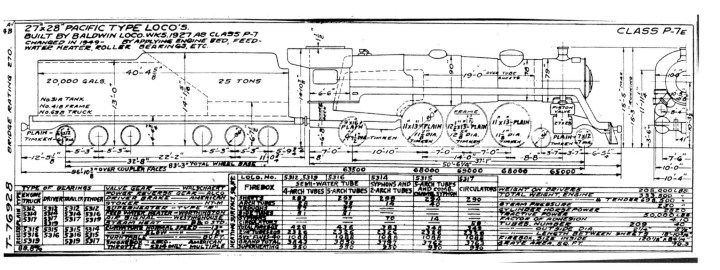

Class P-7 Pacific 5306, the President Van Buren, departs Jersey City, N.J., on Jersey Central tracks with a west-bound passenger train in this undated photo. The P-7 class locomotives originally were painted in olive green with gold stripes that were bordered in maroon. The box on the pilot held automatic train control equipment, which was required for operation on the Reading and CNJ railroads. (TLC Collection)

Class P-7 Pacific 5316, now painted blue with no presidential name, relaxes under the coal dock in Toledo, Ohio, in 1950. In earlier times, the locomotive was named for President Grant. (Bernard Kern photo, TLC Collection)

Class P-7 Pacific 5311, the President Fillmore, takes Train 2, the eastbound National Limited, across the Thomas Viaduct at Relay, Md., in about 1936. Originally an all-Pullman train, by this time coaches are being permitted to hobnob with the sleepers. Note that the tender has been fitted with an extended coal bunker and the bell has been moved from the fireman's side to the engineer's side of the boiler, as compared to the engine's as-built configuration. (H.W. Pontin photo, TLC Collection)

The 5316 has aroused from slumber as a hostler blows condensate out of its cylinders preparatory to another run from Toledo in 1950. Maybe the locomotive will head south with The Cincinnatian or south, then east, with the Ambassador. (Bernard Kern photo, TLC Collection)

Class P-7a Pacific 5304 displays its train name proudly in this photo. Streamlining was an effort to attract and hold passengers to revamped trains. In 1939 No. 5304's streamlining was removed and she reverted to class P-7, only to be streamlined again in 1946 for service on The Cincinnatian. The locomotive was retired in 1957 as a streamlined P-7d. The Royal Blue was canceled – along with all other passenger trains running between Jersey City, N.J., and Baltimore – effective with their last trips beginning on Saturday, April 26, 1958. (Bob Withers Collection)

Class P-7c Pacific 5308, the former President Tyler, departs Cincinnati Union terminal with Train 238 for Columbus, Newark, Wheeling and Pittsburgh in April 1956. Soon, as diesels crowd their way into the company's four-digit numbering system, the engine will receive a new number, 106, and take its final trip into history in a year or so. (Herbert H. Harwood Jr. photo, TLC Collection)

It's July 3, 1935, and Class P-7 Pacific 5314 is running through Newark, N.J., on Jersey Central tracks with Train 10, the eastbound Chicago-Pittsburgh-New York Express. The locomotive was one of seven P-7's that were reclassified P-7c when they received cast steel beds, in which the frame, cross braces, cylinders, pilot deck and pump brackets were all one casting. They were given feed-water heaters, smoke-box throttles, larger tenders, and air pumps and after-cooler pipes hidden behind a shield on the pilot that carrying the B&O Capitol Dome emblem. Headlights were repositioned in the center of the smokebox doors with bells placed above them, and classification lamps raised higher. (Jay Williams Collection)

Class P-7 Pacific 5314 – in an undated photo but obviously before the locomotive was modernized and reclassified P-7c – brings Train 1, the westbound National Limited, past F Tower in Washington, D.C. The train will follow the main line around to the train's right to QN Tower and back into Washington Union Station. (B&O Railroad Historical Society Collection)

Here is a sign of things to come – it's July 20, 1947, and Class P-7 Pacific 5316 is being led by a two-unit diesel. Class DP-2 [model EA] 51 and (probably DP-2x [model EB] 51x) are in the lead as the three locomotives are starting to back Train 1, the westbound National Limited, from QN Tower to Washington, D.C., Union Station. Other photographers are on hand to record the nine-car train – and possibly the diesel/ steam combination – for posterity. (E.L. Thompson photo, B&O Railroad Historical Society Collection)

Class P-7b Pacific 5306 charges through Collingdale, Pa., with Train 3, the westbound Diplomat, on Oct. 1, 1944. The engine, originally a P-7, was reclassified in 1942 when it received a company-designed Type R superheater with a special plate on top of the smokebox. (Charles A. Brown photo, TLC Collection)

This photo offers a good broadside view of a P-7 Pacific. Engine 5307 takes a sunbath beside a PRR GG-1 in Washington, D.C.'s Ivy City engine terminal on June 5, 1947. No. 5307 is one of only four P-7's that were never rebuilt into one of the later P-7 sub-classes. (L.W. Rice photo, TLC Collection)

This photo shows the appearance of a P-7 locomotive after it was modernized and reclassified P-7c. Engine 5305 brings Train 246 into Wheeling, W.Va., on June 28, 1956. In the distance, we can see either Train 233 to Cincinnati or Train 73 to Kenova, W.Va., departing. (Charles W. Aurand photo, Bob Withers Collection)

Opposite: Class P-7d Pacific 5301 charges up Cheat River Grade and crosses the Tray Run Viaduct west of Rowlesburg, W.Va., with Train 75, the westbound Cincinnatian, on July 26, 1949. The train was limited to five rebuilt heavyweight cars to enable it to keep its speedy 12½-hour schedule, but the restriction prevented adding coaches as demand warranted and eventually forced the company to switch the train to the flatter Cincinnati-Detroit route in 1950, where more cars could be added to the consist. (R.H. Kindig photo, TLC Collection)

Opposite Below: Class P-7d Pacific 5304 is handling an unusual assignment in 1948, taking a 20-car trainload of displays to the Chicago Railroad Fair. The train is pulling out of a siding at Silver Spring, Md. (Bruce D. Fales photo, B&O Railroad Historical Society Collection)

Below: Class P-7d Pacific 5301 is pulling out of Toledo, Ohio, on Oct. 11, 1956, with Train 53, the southbound Cincinnatian, on its final steam-powered run. The engine will receive a new number, 109, in February 1957, and will go to scrap later that year. With all that black exhaust, it looks like the 5301 is spewing one final act of defiance intended for the diesel locomotives that will replace it. (John A. Rehor photo, TLC collection)

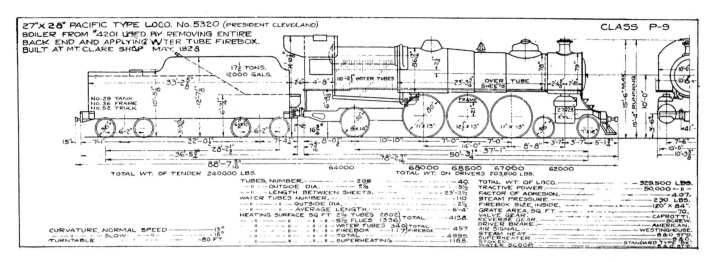

27"x28" PACIFIC TYPE LOCO. No. 5320 (PRESIDENT CLEVELAND)
BOILER FROM #4201 USED BY REMOVING ENTIRE
BACK END AND APPLYING WATER TUBE FIREBOX.
BUILT AT MT. CLARE SHOP MAY, 1928

CLASS P-9

TOTAL WT. OF TENDER 240000 LBS.
TOTAL WT. ON DRIVERS 203,600 LBS.

CURVATURE, NORMAL SPEED — 13°
" " SLOW " — 18°
TURNTABLE — 80 FT.

TUBES, NUMBER.	205
" " OUTSIDE DIA.	2½
" " LENGTH BETWEEN SHEETS.	23'-3½
WATER TUBES NUMBER.	110
" " " OUTSIDE DIA.	2½
" " " AVERAGE LENGTH.	6'-4
HEATING SURFACE SQ FT 2½ TUBES 2802	
" " " 5½ FLUES 1336 TOTAL	4138
" " " WATER TUBES 340 TOTAL	
" " " FIREBOX 117 FIREBOX	457
" " " TOTAL	4595
" " " SUPERHEATING.	1188
	40
TOTAL WT. OF LOCO.	329,500 LBS.
TRACTIVE POWER.	50,000 " "
FACTOR OF ADHESION.	4.07
STEAM PRESSURE.	230 LBS.
FIREBOX SIZE, INSIDE.	120" X 84"
GRATE AREA, SQ. FT.	70
VALVE GEAR.	CAPROTTI
REVERSE GEAR.	SCREW
DRIVER BRAKE.	AMERICAN
AIR SIGNAL.	WESTINGHOUSE
STEAM HEAT.	B&O STD.
SUPERHEATER.	
STOKER.	STANDARD TYPE
WATER SCOOP.	

In May, 1928, just more than a year after the last P-7 was delivered, the company's Mount Clare shops built another Pacific, No. 5320, class P-9, President Cleveland. This was a very different locomotive, equipped with a massive water tube firebox. Despite its very different appearance, the P-9 was very similar in overall dimensions and performance to the P-7. It was built using the boiler shell from Mikado No. 4201, with the firebox removed and replaced by the watertube firebox. It appears that the trailing truck from the Mikado was also used. The P-9 was also equipped, as an experiment, with Caprotti poppet valves. The builders also made every effort to hide as many of the appliances as possible, giving the locomotive a very sleek appearance.

Top: B&O Railroad diagram for the P-9 as originally built.

This page center: B&O photo of No. 5320 as she was originally built. Note the lack of conventional valve gear and the squared off steam chest above the cylinders, both indicators of the presence of the Caprotti poppet valves. These valves apparently were not a success, in that the railroad removed them in 1929, replacing them with conventional piston valves and Walschaerts valve gear, and changing the class to P-9a. (B&O Railroad photo, collection of Edwin C. Kirstatter)

Opposite Top: This is how P-9a No. 5320 looked after the poppet valves were removed and replaced with standard piston valves and Walschaerts valve gear in 1929. Note that the appliances are still mostly hidden. (B&O Railroad photo, TLC Collection)

Opposite Center: P-9a No. 5320 is seen on November 6th of 1937 at the B&O station at 24th & Chestnut in Philadelphia, Pa., being attached to Train 13's baggage car. The fireman is on the deck of its new replacement tender that looks like the P-1d type. He may be going to water it from the nearby penstock. Two other crewman are riding on the front steps of engine. (W.R.Osborne photo, collection of Edwin C. Kirstatter.)

Opposite Bottom: No. 5320 still has its capped stack and original tender with additional coal boards bringing the capacity up to 19½ tons. The train control equipment box is still on the pilot deck as required on the eastern divisions, but the ladders are now a more standard type. Before the air compressor was nowhere to be seen and now it is up on the running boards on this side of engines boiler. The electric generator is now on top of the smokebox in front of the stack relocated from perhaps on the tender deck out of sight before. (Edwin C. Kirstatter collection)

In 1945 the No. 5320's watertube firebox was removed and the engine rebuilt into a standard P-7 Pacific, all be it one sporting a Boxpok main driver and lagging on the smokebox. (TLC Collection)

P-7 No. 5320, the former P-9 President Cleveland, is seen here on Train 233 at Columbus Union Station in Columbus, Ohio, on April 24, 1954. (Donald A. Kaiser photo, Alex Campbell Collection)

The nine cars of train No. 11, The Metropolitan Special, with P-7 No. 5320 on the head end, is at Hancock, W. Va., on March 16, 1947. (E.L. Thompson photo, B&O RR Historical Society Collection)

The ultimate P-7's were the streamlined P-7d's and the P-7e's. These engines were equipped with cast steel engine beds, roller bearings on all axles, feedwater heaters, and air pumps mounted on the pilot deck behind a shield. Tenders were of 20,000-gallon capacity, with a coal capacity of 23 tons on the P-7d and 25 tons on the P-7e. Some engines were also equipped with Boxpok drivers, as seen here on P-7e No. 5314. (TLC Collection)

The engineer of Train No. 34 is leaving Harpers Ferry, W.Va., in a big hurry, crossing the bridge over the Potomac River into Maryland. P-7e No. 5315 will lead its train into Washington, D.C., making a good dozen stops along the way. (James P. Gallagher photo, TLC Collection)

P-7c No. 5317 rolls through a snowy Tacoma Park, Md., on December 10, 1948, with the nine cars of Train No. 21, The Washingtonian. The box that is mounted under the running board just ahead of the air tank is the hot water pump for the engine's Worthington feedwater heater. (Jay Williams Collection)

P-7c No. 5317 is seen again, this time with Train No. 5 at Collingdale, Pa., on December 14, 1946. (TLC Collection)

Inherited Pacifics

As the B&O acquired other railroads, their locomotives were merged into the B&O's locomotive classification scheme and they were assigned B&O locomotive numbers. Mergers which included Pacific type locomotives included:

- The Cincinnati, Hamilton and Dayton, merged with the B&O in December, 1917.

- The Cincinnati, Indianapolis and Western, leased to the B&O in May, 1927.

- The Buffalo, Rochester and Pittsburgh, merged with the B&O on January 1, 1932.

The B&O acquired control of the Chicago & Alton Railroad in July, 1931, renaming it the Alton Railroad, but not merging it into the larger B&O. The Alton was operated separately under B&O control, but its locomotives were assigned classes and numbers in the B&O system. The Alton went into bankruptcy in 1941 and was merged with the Gulf, Mobile and Ohio Railroad in June, 1947, ending its connection with the B&O. Since the Alton was never merged with the B&O, we are only presenting a summary of its Pacific locomotives here, rather than a detailed roster.

Summary of Alton Pacifics		
Class	Number	Quantity
P-10	5265	1
P-11	5266	1
P-12	5267-5269	3
P-13	5270-5274	5
P-14	5275-5279	5
P-15	5280-5289	10
P-16	5290-5299	10
Alton was controlled by the B&O from July 1931 to June 1947, when it was sold to and merged into the Gulf, Mobile, and Ohio.		

P-2a No. 5095, formerly CH&D No. 501, with a train at College Corner, Ohio sometime in the '30s or '40s. It's been given a dumping tender. (Max Miller photo, Bob Withers Collection)

Inherited Pacifics Roster							
Class	Original Owner's No.	Number	Original Owner	Original Class	Built	Retired	Notes
P-2	501	5095	CH&D	P	Jun-10	Oct-47	all were reclassified to P-2a when super-heated.
P-2	502	5096			Jun-10	Nov-46	All built by Alco-Schenectady
P-2	503	5097			Jun-10	Dec-47	CH&D acquired by B&O in December, 1917
P-2	504	5098			Jun-10	Jan-48	
P-2	505	5099			Jun-10	Nov-47	
P-8	121	5196	CI&W		Oct-24	Oct-51	all built by Alco-Brooks
P-8	122	5197			Oct-24	Oct-51	CI&W leased to B&O in May, 1927
P-8	123	5198			Oct-24	Nov-51	
P-8	124	5199			Oct-24	Oct-51	
P-17	600	5140-5148	BR&P	WW	Feb-12	Aug-51	BR&P merged into B&O on January 1, 1932.
P-17	601	5141			Feb-12	1947	All built by Alco-Brooks
P-17	602	5142			Feb-12	Aug-51	
P-17a	603	5143			Feb-13	Oct-51	
P-17a	604	5144			Jul-13	Mar-50	
P-17a	605	5145			Jul-13	Feb-53	
P-17a	606	5146			Jul-13	Apr-52	
P-17a	607	5147			Jun-14	Apr-52	
P-17a	608	5148			Jun-14	Jan-53	
P-18	609	5185	BR&P	WW	Jan-18	Apr-52	All built by Alco-Brooks
P-18	610	5186			Jan-18	Apr-52	
P-18	611	5187			Jan-18	Dec-52	
P-18a	612	5188			Jun-18	1945	
P-18a	613	5189			Jun-18	Apr-52	
P-18a	614	5190			Jun-18	Apr-52	
P-18a	615	5191			Jun-18	Apr-52	
P-18a	616	5192			Jun-18	Oct-52	
P-19	675	5260	BR&P	WW2	Aug-23	May-52	All built by Alco-Brooks
P-19	676	5261			Aug-23	Jun-51	
P-19	677	5262			Aug-23	May-52	
P-19	678	5263			Aug-23	Apr-52	
P-19	679	5264			Aug-23	May-52	
Class P-2 was first numbered 2175 – 2170 on the B&O, then renumberd to 5090 – 5094, then renumbered to 5095 – 5099.							

Class P-8 Pacific 5196 began life as Cincinnati, Indianapolis & Western 121. The location is unknown, but if that is the Western Hills Viaduct above the tender, then it's Cincinnati. Alco's Brooks Works built the locomotive in October 1924. The CI&W became part of the B&O in May 1927, and the 5196 was sold for scrap in October 1951. (Max Miller photo, Bob Withers Collection)

Alton P-16 No. 5292 with the southbound Abraham Lincoln near Chicago circa 1939. (Paul M. Moffitt photo, Jay Williams Collection)

It's 9:05 on a sunny morning in 1950, and Class P-17 Pacific 5140 is departing Smithfield Street Station in Pittsburgh with coach-only Train 254 for Buffalo, N.Y. Alco's Brooks Works built the locomotive for the Buffalo, Rochester & Pittsburgh in February 1912 and it was assigned the number 600 in BR&P's WW class. BR&P became B&O's Buffalo Division in January 1932. The locomotive was scrapped in August 1951. (Herbert H. Harwood Jr. photo, TLC Collection)

The Great Lakes Express is in Pittsburgh, Pa., with P-17a No. 5145 (former BR&P No. 605) in 1933. (Jay Williams Collection)

Class P-17 No. 5143 and Class P No. 5053 double-head mail and express train No. 31 at Rockville, Md. in March, 1946. (Bruce D. Fales photo, Jay Williams Collection)

Class P-17a Pacific 5146 is doing the honors as Train 254 at Punxsutawney, Pa., on Saturday, July 28, 1951, at 12:37 p.m. if the train is on time. Anybody know the make and model of that closest automobile? (John F. Humiston photo, TLC Collection)

Class P-17a Pacific 5146 with the same train on the same day as in the photo on the opposite page, but a bit earlier, in Butler, Pa. If the coach-only train is on time, it's 10:40 a.m. Alco's Brooks Works built the engine in July 1913 as Buffalo, Rochester & Pittsburgh 606. B&O took over the BR&P in January 1932, and the engine was sold for scrap in April 1952. (John F. Humiston photo, TLC Collection)

Class P-18 Pacific 5185 takes a breather at East Salamanca, N.Y., on Aug. 2, 1949. Alco's Brooks Works built the engine for the Buffalo, Rochester & Pittsburgh in January 1918 as its Class WW 609. B&O sold the locomotive for scrap in April 1952. (Bruce D. Fales photo, Jay Williams Collection)

"POTUS" Pacifics

Several B&O Pacifics are known to have served their country by pulling POTUS (acrostic for "President of the United States") trains.

Among them was a funeral train for Warren G. Harding, who died in San Francisco on the way back from driving a gold spike to complete the Alaska Railroad. Now the railroad cars that took him westward would return to the East as a funeral train. B&O received the train in Chicago on Aug. 6, 1923, for an overnight trip to Washington, D.C.

The locomotive that pulled the train from Chicago to Garrett, Ind., is unknown to the author, but from that point Class P-6 5233 forwarded it to Willard, Ohio; Class P-5a 5224 to Glenwood Yard (Pittsburgh), Class P-1aa 5052 to Cumberland, Md., and Class P-5 5217 to Washington. After Harding's body lay in state for public viewing and a funeral service at the U.S. Capitol, the Pennsylvania and Erie railroads forwarded it to Marion, Ohio, for burial.

Several Class P-5, P-5a, and P-7 Pacifics pulled POTUS trains for Franklin D. Roosevelt. Class P-7 5308 took FDR from Jersey City, N.J., to Washington on April 21, 1933, and Class P-7 5313 forwarded him across the same territory on the night of July 6-7, 1937. That train pulled into a siding at Fort George G. Meade Junction for about an hour and a half so arrival at Union Station would not occur before 8:30 a.m.

Eight B&O Pacifics took part in a secret national tour arranged in 1943 so the president could inspect wartime military facilities and manufacturing plants. Class P-7 5319 had the easiest job – forwarding the train from its point of origin in Silver Spring, Md., to Washington Union Station's lower level – 6.9 miles in 18 minutes with seven cars. Actually, the president and the two rear cars – Pullman 8-compartment/lounge *Conneaut* for the Secret Service and armor-plated Pullman private car *Ferdinand Magellan* for Roosevelt – weren't added to the train until after the Richmond, Fredericksburg & Potomac locomotive took over for the first southward leg of the trip. The other seven engines hauled the president eastward on the night of April 28-29, 1943, after Roosevelt had completed his inspections: P-5a 5206 and P-5 5207 from Louisville to Cincinnati, P-5a's 5228 and 5213 to Chillicothe, Ohio, P-5a's 5218 and 5213 to Grafton, W.Va., and Class P-7 5313 from Keyser, W.Va., to Washington.

Class P-5 5209 had the softest time of all her sisters. A PRR engine brought the rear three cars of Roosevelt's campaign train from the siding under the U.S. Bureau of Engraving and Printing on the night of Oct. 26, 1944, and took them to Anacostia Junction, D.C. The 5209 forwarded the cars from Anacostia Junction, D.C., to Alexandria Junction, Md., all of 6.3 miles, to meet up with a diesel that that brought the front 10 cars from Union Station. Thus ended the 5209's role in the movement.

As far as we know, none of the B&O locomotives used to haul Roosevelt's trains were decorated – and that would certainly be true of his secret wartime movements. So we will concentrate on the engines that were decorated for Harding's funeral train.

Properly draped Class P-6 Pacific 5233 stands ready at Garrett, Ind., on Aug. 6, 1923, for its solemn assignment of pulling Warren Harding's funeral train to Willard, Ohio. (Robert W. Parker photo, B&O Railroad Museum Collection)

Class P-5 Pacific 5224 slowly forwards Warren Harding's funeral train past the crowd below Machinery Hall at Carnegie Tech – now Carnegie Mellon University – in Oakland, Pa.'s Junction Hollow, west of Pittsburgh, on the morning of Aug. 7, 1923. Note the people standing on the steps of Schenley (SC) Tower beside the train's fourth car. (John J. Consoli Collection, Bob Withers Collection)

Curious and grieving crowds have surrounded the main line at Glenwood, east of Pittsburgh, as engine 5224 brings Warren Harding's funeral train into town on Aug. 7, 1923. Another locomotive will take over from here. (Alvin K. Barr photo, B&O Railroad Museum Collection)

Above: Class P-1aa Pacific 5052 may be easing through Connellsville, Pa., with Warren Harding's funeral train on Aug. 7, 1923. The engineer is looking back at his train, so the train may be standing still for some reason. (Smithsonian Institution, Bob Withers Collection)

Opposite Top: The engineer and fireman going on duty at Cumberland, Md., on Aug. 7, 1923, pose with Class P-5 Pacific 5217, which will forward Warren Harding's funeral train to Washington, D.C. (Alvin K. Barr photo, B&O Railroad Museum Collection)

Opposite Bottom: The engineer has oiled around and taken his seat on the right side of the 5217's cab, but takes the time to pose for yet another picture before he couples to Warren Harding's funeral train in Cumberland, Md., on Aug. 7, 1923. (Alvin K. Barr photo, B&O Railroad Museum Collection)

Class P-5 Pacific 5217 has coupled to Warren Harding's funeral train in Cumberland, Md., on Aug. 7, 1923. Three children sitting on the rail are gathering memories for a lifetime – which may be cut short if they don't get up before the next train comes down the track upon which they are trespassing. (Smithsonian Institution, Bob Withers Collection)

This view offers a better look at the front of Class P-5 Pacific 5217 as it gets ready to depart Cumberland, Md., with Warren Harding's funeral train on Aug. 7, 1923. (Library of Congress, Bob Withers Collection)

A Pacific Album

We think this train is being pulled by a P-1 Pacific, but we don't know which one or what sub-class. The train is Grafton-Wheeling, W.Va., Train 343 (No. 430 beyond Moundsville), which has just popped out of Sales Tunnel on May 1, 1953. At the time, the train carried a reclining-seat coach with lunch counter and lounge rooms and a 10-section/2-compartment/1-drawing room sleeper from Washington, D.C., having been forwarded on Train 23 to Grafton. The tunnel was a mile and a half west of Hundred, W.Va., 44.5 rail miles from Wheeling. If the train is on time, it's about 8 a.m. (O.V. Nelson photo, Bob Withers Collection)

Class P-5a Pacific 5220 spends some down time with other locomotives at the Benwood, W.Va., engine servicing facility in June 1954. This engine was a bit unique on the B&O in that, unlike most Pacifics on the railroad, she was built by Alco rather than Baldwin. The 5220 was the final engine of its class to remain in service; it was retired in October 1956. (J.J. Young Jr. photo, Bob Withers Collection)

Not only is the P-7 Pacific in this photo unidentified, we also don't know what train it's pulling. The train is westbound, just a short distance from the Union Station in Akron, Ohio, going through the JO Interlocker, and is about to cross the Erie's two track main on the right and then pass under the Mill Street Overpass bridge. This is a joint operation with the PRR from Akron Junction to Warwick and the westbound track is owned by the B&O. The date of December 1949 is written on the back of the print, but timetables for that period don't show any locals, which this train appears to be. Isn't it a nice picture? (TLC Collection)

It's nearly 10:50 a.m. on a clear day in June 1954 as engineer Roy Roush checks his timepiece on the head end of coach-only Wheeling-Kenova, W.Va., Train 73 just before departure on Wheeling's elevated station tracks. Most likely his engine is a P-5, P-5a or P-6a Pacific. Roush retired later that year – the night trains between Wheeling and Kenova had been dropped the previous year, and diesels were on the way. The old hogger probably figured that railroading in the years ahead wouldn't be as much fun. (J.J. Young Jr. photo, Bob Withers Collection)

Charleston-Grafton, W.Va., Train 36 is crossing the Tygart Valley River as it enters Grafton just before 2:35 p.m. on Oct. 17, 1947, if it's on time. An equipment listing in the timetable for that date shows that passengers were offered no amenities for the seven-hour trip. (B&O Railroad Historical Society, TLC Collection)

Class Pc No. 5176. Sadly, no location or date is given, although the overhead wire in the background suggests that the location is near the Ivy City engine terminal in Washington D.C., and the time is sometime after 1935, when the Pennsylvania RR put in its electrification into Washington. (C. W. Witbeck photo, TLC Collection)

An unidentified Pacific on the point of Pittsburgh-Columbus Train 33 has just exited Tunnel No. 1 and is crossing Wheeling Creek a little over a mile east of the Wheeling, W.Va., station in February 1946. If the train is on time, it's about 10:20 a.m. The train featured an individual-seat coach and parlor-dining car for Cincinnati and another individual-seat coach with a lunch counter for Parkersburg, W.Va., that it handed off to Train 73 at Wheeling. (J.J. Young Jr. photo, Bob Withers Collection)

P-6a No. 5244 on Train 73, at the left, and P-1aa No. 5057 on Train 33, at the right, wait at the station in Wheeling, W. Va., in September 1945. (J. J. Young photo, Bob Withers Collection)

P-7b No. 5306 in a nice portrait view. (TLC Collection)

P-5a No. 5218 strikes a pose on the turntable at Washington, Ind., on June 20, 1955. This view clearly shows the taller pilot steps, lengthened to clear the drifting valves on the top of the steam chest, as well as the Capitol Dome plate at the center of the smokebox, as well as the graphite on the smokebox front and firebox sides. (TLC Collection)

P-5 No. 5229 has been specially lettered for an outing of the Holy Name Society. Seen here at Riverside roundhouse in Baltimore in 1937. (B&O Railroad photo, TLC Collection)

On July 27, 1947, *The Cincinnatian is in the charge of P-7c No. 5317 rather than one of the streamlined P-7d's that were purpose rebuilt for this train. Here it is crossing the Tygart Valley River in Grafton, W. Va., westbound to the train's name-sake city. (R. H. Kindig photo, TLC Collection)*

P-3 No. 5128 had exchanged her original dumping tender for a conventional one by the time she was photographed with Train 62 on the Allingdale Branch in West Virginia. (Bruce D. Fales photo, Jay Williams Collection)

Train No. 19, the westbound Ambassador, with P-7c No. 5318 steams through a snowy Berwyn, Md., on February 28, 1949. (Bruce D. Fales photo, Jay Williams Collection)

A "special" train with P-7 No. 5308, President Taylor, and 9 CNJ coaches passing F Tower in Washington, D. C., on a very cold January 10, 1940. (Bruce D. Fales photo, Jay Williams Collection)

Train 28, The Columbian, with P-7 No. 5317, President Pierce, and 7 cars leaves Washington, D. C. for Jersey City, N.J., on September 4, 1938. (Bruce D. Fales photo, Jay Williams Collection)

93

P-7d No. 5302 on display at the Chicago Railroad Fair in 1949. Note the EM-1 2-8-8-4
freight engine behind the Pacific, and the power unit for the ACF Talgo train on the right.
(TLC Colleciton)

P-5 No. 5225 with Train 12 takes water in Chilicothe, Ohio, in December 1941. (H. R.
Blackburn photo, Jay Williams Collection)

P-6a No. 5240, double-headed with another Pacific, departs Garrett, Ind., with the Fort Pitt Limited circa 1930. (Bob Graham photo, Jay Williams Collection

*No. 5003 with eastbound Train 22, the east-
~d Washingtonian, is leaving the P&LE station
~tsburgh in December 1949. (H. H. Harwood
~, TLC Collection)*

Train No. 2, The National Limited, is eastbound behind P-7 No. 5300, President Washington, at Elizabethport, N.J., on March 22, 1937. No. 5300 is the only surviving P&O Pacific, now on display at the B&O Museum in Baltimore. (George E. Votava photo, TLC Collection)

P-7c No. 5308 leads a train at Columbus, Ohio, in 1950. (Bernard Kern photo, TLC Collection)

Southbound Train 53, The Great Lakes Limited, with P-5 No. 5212 on the head end, on the Delray Crossing in Detroit, Mich., on April 12, 1950. (Elmer Treloar photo, TLC Collection)